# Ro-Hun Therapy

The Greatest
Transformational Process
of Our Time

## Janice Hayes
*Doctor of Ro-Hun Therapy*

DENVER, COLORADO

Ro-Hun Therapy
The Greatest Transformational Process of Our Time
All Rights Reserved.
Copyright © 2013 Janice Hayes
v4.0

Ro-Hun is a registered trademark for Ro-Hun Therapy

Outskirts Press, Inc.
http://www.outskirtspress.com

ISBN: 978-1-4787-0989-3

Library of Congress Control Number: 2013906814

Outskirts Press and the "OP" logo are trademarks belonging to Outskirts Press, Inc.

PRINTED IN THE UNITED STATES OF AMERICA

*For Kristy.*
*You are the brightest star*
*in my Universe.*

"We are not human beings
living a spiritual life.

We are spiritual beings
living a human life."

-Pierre Tielhard de Chardin

# Table of Contents

# *Introduction*

I am a Ro-Hun therapist. More specifically, I am a Doctor and Instructor of Ro-Hun Therapy. Ro-Hun Therapy is a healing process that enables us to uncover and rectify beliefs and ideas that confine us to patterns of repetitious, painful behaviors. The purpose of Ro-Hun therapy—a non-traditional, alternative approach to self-understanding and healing—is to free us to live life as vibrant, spiritually-aware human beings. This book will introduce you to this amazing, effective, and life-transforming process. While Ro-Hun has existed since the early 1980s, relatively few people are aware of it. Therefore, Ro-Hun therapy is probably the best-kept healing secret of our time. And now, it is time for this enlightened process of healing to be made known.

As with many great things, Ro-Hun Therapy came about simply, with very little fanfare. Its developments, scope, and power have only grown and deepened over time as those who facilitate the process have discovered. In 1983, while in meditation, Patricia Hayes, founder of Delphi University, a school of healing and spiritual practices, met an individual who called himself "Dr. Ro-Hun." Patricia had been working in the area of spiritual growth and development for over 20 years, so this person's appearance and desire to communicate with her was not unusual. He introduced himself, saying that "Ro" was his name and "Hun" his profession. He explained to Patricia that while he did not currently exist on the physical plane, the central theme of his existence and work was to help humans heal their faulty thoughts. He found in Patricia a willing and skillful channel for the information he was ready to share. She named the resulting process after him, Ro-Hun Therapy, and thus, a new and exciting personal transformative process was quietly born.

The basis of Ro-Hun Therapy was, and remains today, the discovery of the destructive partnerships of faulty thoughts and negative feelings that we hold within us. For the most part, these partnerships are hidden within our consciousness and they direct the flow of our lives, even without our knowledge of their existence. It has taken centuries to discover and name truths and principles that have always been functioning. For example, we knew things fell "down" and didn't fall "up," but we didn't know why. Then, Newton was hit on the head by an apple and discerned the principle of gravitational force. Similarly, our personal lives have troubles, failures, and recurring problems, and we don't know why. We blame others for them, but in reality, there is a principle involved: *What I think about myself and how I feel about myself is how I behave*. Dr. Ro-Hun dropped this apple of awareness into Patricia Hayes' receptive consciousness, and our knowledge of ourselves as the creators of our lives has expanded exponentially. Faulty thoughts and negative feelings are dictating human life with or without our knowledge of them.

True to her nature, Patricia began to work immediately with the information she was given. She was so excited about the potential and wanted to share it with others. She knew that I was interested in this kind of healing and called me and filled me in on what she was discovering. Without hesitation, I flew from California to North Carolina to participate. My experience was nothing short of amazing.

Based on trust, we participants listened, learned, and stumblingly practiced on each other. With each step, we knew *something* was happening, because each of us experienced profound openings. The process was raw and forming—that much was clear—but even in that embryonic state, it was effective. I took my scanty, jumbled notes home to California and offered what I had learned to clients. Without exception, each one left the sessions with a healthier experience of themselves, some deeper than others, to be true, but all were affected positively. No one was more surprised than I was because the changes came so relatively easily. Like everyone else in the world at that time, I knew therapy to be a time-consuming process. Psychoanalysis and psychotherapy happened in terms of years. Yet, there we were, making changes in terms of *hours*, and these changes appeared to have a lasting effect. I was hooked. The clients kept coming and each one left glowing with new life, new prospects, new understanding, and new power.

Patricia made it clear that we were continually researching the process. Over time and through practice, application, and Patricia's communications with Dr. Ro-Hun, the original process was refined and new processes were developed. Approaches changed, matured, and deepened as Ro-Hun continued to evolve and expand through the years, and the healing results followed suit. Today, Ro-Hun is a deep, powerful, cohesive, effective whole.

When I moved to McCaysville, Georgia, in 1997, to join the staff of Delphi University, I became a Ro-Hun instructor. A Zen saying states, "*If you want to learn, read. If you want to know, write. If you want to master, teach.*" I was on the Ro-Hun fast track. As a Ro-Hun therapist in my own practice, I was privy to profound changes in clients. As an instructor, I not only saw the clients change, advance, and heal, but I witnessed the evolution of my student therapists as well. I watched as new therapists-in-training entered the program, and within the first two classes, they evolved from uncertain "who, me?" attitudes to a deeper understanding and personal confidence.

We practitioners of Ro-Hun Therapy are highly dedicated and skilled, but we are not sanctioned through the traditional mainstream educational process. We have taken the path less travelled in our search for spiritual awareness and personal transformation. We come from all lifestyles and all socio-economic groups, covering the field in terms of occupation and interests—from housewives, farmers, and school bus drivers, to artists, musicians, and teachers. We include engineers, construction workers, computer geeks, and military personnel. Some of us are traditionally trained psychologists, psychotherapists, and psychiatrists, who have discovered that Ro-Hun is a faster and more effective form of mental and emotional healing than many traditional processes. Some of us are medical doctors already participating in or seeking to study alternative healing methods. We are men and women, youthful and mature individuals, with families, friends, jobs, and lives that look just like everyone else's. We live in many countries around the world, we speak many languages, and we come from varying spiritual backgrounds. What we have in common is our deep desire to live a spiritual life—one based on wisdom and love with a deep, personal connection to our Divine Source. We want to live an awake and aware life. We also want to help others find their peace and wholeness so that all of us can live more fully, freely, and abundantly, contributing to the health of the planet and its people.

Ro-Hun is about miracles. Miracles are rapidly occurring events based on natural principles. Every client and every therapist experiences miracles. They are part of the landscape of Ro-Hun and they become habitual—that is, as a therapist, we *expect* them to happen because they do. The miracles encompass the whole of the human being: physical, mental/emotional, and spiritual, because Ro-Hun is a holistic therapy.

In some cases, the results appear quite dramatically in the body. I had a client who lived with migraines. They were part of her daily life and nothing touched them; she had learned how to suffer quietly. During the third session of the process called "Purification," in one moment, in one realization of a faulty thought she had been carrying for years—"*I am responsible for everybody*"—the migraine that she was experiencing while we worked ceased and has never returned, even several years later.

A Ro-Hun student who was on campus for part of her doctoral training, Constructs and Vaults, had a huge breakthrough while being a client during a student practice session. She awoke the next morning to find her severely weak eyesight, which she had lived with all her life, dramatically improved. Physical healing is, more often than not, a process, rather than an event. The migraine healing occurred after two sessions; the eyesight healing occurred after many sessions and two years of study. Throughout the entire scope of the Ro-Hun processes, from Purification to Tanks, the body is the happy recipient of healthy, glowing, positive thoughts, and feelings, which result in a more vibrant life and responsive body.

All miracles originate at the emotional/mental level because that level affects the physical body directly. Lives have been transformed from this level. I have seen clients and students alike attain such depth of understanding and forgiveness that they have forever altered the ways in which they develop and behave in relationships. Those who needed to break free of toxic relationships were able to do so. Those who wanted to retain relationships in healthier ways did so. Others were able to find the kind of relationship they had been seeking. Still others were able to forgive their abusers and walk away from years of painful, buried memories. Without exception, they accomplished these relationship miracles with love and understanding, ending forever the blame, shame, and pain.

Spiritually, all miracles already exist, waiting to be expressed when the mental/emotional level releases the painful thoughts and feelings that block them. I remember well a man who had lived with the idea that he had to work hard and struggle to be successful. He felt alone in the world—in spite of having a lovely family—because he *believed* he was alone without anyone to share his burdens.

"It's what men do," he said to me one day.

Then, as we worked on releasing his entire body of belief that struggle and isolation were foregone conclusions of life, he had a moment with God. In a nanosecond, I saw the truth dawn on his face. In that moment, he was home in love and oneness. He felt it. He *knew* it, and it was more real for him than the belief in isolation used to be. He changed right there on the healing table—his state of bliss shining on his face as pure illumination.

Is Ro-Hun right for everybody? Not at all. Those who benefit the most are those who have a deep desire to find peace and wholeness; they are ready to take an honest look at themselves, and they are willing to admit to the damaging thoughts and emotional pain they carry in secret. They are ready to open themselves to the power of their Spirit to help them release their pain and find full, flourishing lives.

Each chapter explains a specific process of Ro-Hun, giving you a picture of the depth and scope of the therapy. From the first process, Purification, to the final process, Tanks, you will be on a journey through the human psyche—a journey that is simultaneously intricate and simple, leading to nothing short of transformation.

Blessings of Light!

# CHAPTER 1

## The Grave of Buried Feelings

We are about to delve into one of the most astonishing secrets of today: *There is a fast track to living a spiritually connected life of fulfillment and wholeness.* This fast track doesn't require years of struggle or living in a cave on a mountaintop. You don't have to take vows of poverty or abstinence. There are no required chants or prayers, no rituals or attendance requirements. However, you must want to be free—free to live a spiritually enhanced life filled with goodness and satisfaction. Not a bad requirement! To understand how Ro-Hun Therapy can open the door to a spiritually satisfying life, we need to understand what a spiritual life looks like and then discover what prevents us from living it.

In our core, each of us is a soul, an individualized spark of the Divine Source. In this book, the terms "soul" or "higher self" are used to refer to this Divine Essence of the human, and the terms "personality" or "ego" refer to the part of us that responds when our name is called. Just as our bodies are composed of our parents' DNA, our Souls are composed of our Divine Parent's Divine Aspects. There are five Divine Aspects:

Love = kindness, caring, connection, acceptance, and unity
Wisdom = discernment, confidence, balance, and knowledge
Harmony = peace, wholeness, integration, and dynamic movement
Beauty = radiance, positive attraction, and inspiration

Understanding = perception, clarity, knowing, and reason

Your spiritual nature is not as far away as it might seem. Every time you feel confidence, for example, you are express-ing your Wisdom; whenever you are kind, your Love is shining through. At one time or another, you have inspired someone and at that moment, your Beauty was evident. Unfortunately, we don't seem to be able to consistently express our Divine Aspects in everyday life. All that is left to express, then, are their oppo-sites, and that results in the following:

Lack of Love = fear, anxiety, isolation, and coldness
Lack of Wisdom = inflexible thinking, poor decisions and choices, and insensitivity
Lack of Harmony = discord (i.e., stress, illness, pain, and disease)
Lack of Beauty = low self-esteem, self-criticism, shyness, and withdrawal
Lack of Understanding = judgment, hostility, condem-nation, and superiority

As much as we would like to say the problems lie outside of us, the world cannot prevent our goodness. The prevention of our goodness happens when we entertain personal ideas and feelings that are the opposite of the Divine Aspects. For example, when you think you are not as good as others are (low self-es-teem, self-criticism), you are shutting down your Beauty. If you dislike others for their differences (judgment, condemnation), you are choosing to turn your back on your Understanding. Any worry and fear will stop Love in its tracks, and making choices that harm you demonstrates a lack of Wisdom. Stress of any kind robs us of Harmony.

External forces will always exist, but we don't have to let those external forces control us. Through healing our personal negative thoughts, Ro-Hun Therapy enables us to connect freely with our spiritual aspect. The visible, tangible results are vision, clarity, purpose, and best of all, the ways and means to navigate this minefield called life.

How does a person know when he or she is ready for this powerful psycho-energetic spiritual therapy? There comes a time in every life when stirrings of dissatisfaction arise. What used to feel right about life just doesn't feel right anymore. What was once interesting or engaging just doesn't have the same "juice" anymore. A sense of restlessness and a desire for something different takes over.

That is the voice of the Soul calling us to awaken.

At first, we interpret dissatisfaction as a problem with a relationship or a job or family. We think a new car or house or wardrobe would make us feel better. We search for any number of feel-good things—shopping or sports or food or a lover. We consider changing jobs or spouses or moving to a different city, or we begin the two-martini lunch along with before-and-after dinner drinks. We might bury ourselves in television or dive into sports as either a participant or a fan; computer games and the Internet might become the drug of choice as we spend hours staring at a little screen. But acquiring and doing those things brings only temporary relief. After a while, we feel empty again, and the unfulfilling search begins anew. What a hamster wheel!

Blame becomes part of our thinking. If he/she/them/they had been different or had done something differently, we'd be better off. We've heard blame coming out the mouths of others, but perhaps we don't recognize our own tendency toward it. It is easy to condemn the government, for example, for our woes and to fault our parents for their failures in raising us. It is very easy to blame our employers for our lack of fulfillment and frighteningly easy to find our spouses liable for our unhappiness. It is not easy, however, to take responsibility for those feelings ourselves.

People have hurt us; this is true. We can recite the times, places, and sometimes even the dates of events that scarred us. But what we often avoid are the ideas and beliefs *we took on about ourselves* because of those events; we remain unaware of the thoughts and feelings we *chose* to hold inside and keep private. These ideas and thoughts become our subtext, running just beneath our conscious mind. Because we are unaware of them, they create and re-create themselves repeatedly in terms of our life's experiences *without us knowing what is happening*. These buried thoughts and feelings—married to deep emotional pain—become what we really believe about ourselves, the things we don't want anyone to know. The thoughts and feelings of failure, helplessness, insecurity, or unworthiness never go away once they are born in us. What we actually do, very skillfully, is push them down so far that we don't have to hear their voices. They are still there, somewhere, inside, and their pain has never dissipated. Worse, however, is that we have created our lives based on them!

For example, as adults, we can remember someone from our childhoods who hurt us. We recall how painful the experience was. Through the years, however, we buried the pain further and further away from our hearts. Yet the burying, ignoring, or denying doesn't erase the pain. It remains in us and continues to poison our beliefs about ourselves even today. The following story is a perfect example of what happens when we bury our pain.

In fourth grade, Bobby made fun of Tommy. He called him "weird" or "stupid," or Bobby laughed at something Tommy said. If we could look inside Tommy at that moment, we would see him recoil in shock and pain. In that inner recoil, he forever captured whatever negative feelings he was having. They remain rigidly inside him, connected to this moment. Maybe he felt ignorant or inferior or very angry and helpless. Right then, Tommy took on an idea about himself. It wasn't happy, and it won't lead him forward into happiness. His thought might have been, "I'm stupid," or "I'm too different," or "I'm ugly," or any one of a 1,001 other thoughts. Whatever the thought was, it wasn't positive, and whatever feelings he had weren't positive ones either. But in that moment, a destructive duo was born: a negative thought about himself married to hurtful feelings.

Tommy moved through his life, knowing he was stupid or too different or ugly, and that knowledge directed his choices. He was too stupid for college, he was too different for social acceptance, and he was too ugly for love. Whatever his life choices were, they were built on a lie. It doesn't take much effort to predict the outcome of these choices—a life of silent futility and quiet despair. Tommy probably knows people, even attends weddings, funerals, Fourth of July parties, but at home alone, in his heart, the futility and despair rise up, and he reaches for the TV remote for the billionth time.

We are all Tommy. We have buried deep inside many, many moments that have little by little become our ideas about ourselves. These personal, painful feelings become like a cesspool (not a far-off metaphor at all) that leaks into us daily. We know this is true because we aren't expressing our Divine Aspects of Love, Wisdom, Beauty, Harmony, and Understanding. We are caught in the opposites of fear, anxiety, stress, judgment, and blame. We've all felt, at one time or another, that the rug was pulled out from under us. In reality, that's exactly what the cesspool does. It keeps returning our own poisonous thoughts and feelings back to us. Because the returning poison is *our own collection of buried thoughts and feelings*, we pull the rug from under our own feet *without knowing it*. Put a series of similar hurtful experiences together, bury them all in a grave of painful feelings deep within, and they truly erode self-esteem. Because once created, they cannot be erased, only transformed.

Ro-Hun brings not only hope to our buried pain, but positive results to our lives. If we open these negative feelings and clean them out, then our lives will no longer be poisoned by past experiences and buried feelings. If Tommy faced the event, if he saw the lie and healed the wound, he could choose a different view of himself and, therefore, build a different life. When we are free from past pain, we are free to create a present and a future built on healthy attitudes, positive feelings, and wholesome self-esteem. This is exactly what Ro-Hun Therapy helps us do.

When we find ourselves spinning on the hamster wheel, the time is actually ripe for us to discover our latent, powerful, and clear spiritual self, which we have put on the back burner. This is when we become sick and tired of being sick and tired. It is time to heal. Part of this healing journey is to reconnect with our Soul, for it is from our Divine Aspects of Love, Wisdom, Beauty, Harmony, and Understanding that we discover our deep well of strength and the truth that we are not helpless. When we are ready, we begin the journey of a thousand steps. How does one start this journey? Follow your own instincts. What do *you* feel will be a way to head for home? Each step leads you forward into another step. You might change direction many times, but if you are willing, each change takes you closer to your Spiritual Self if that is your goal. For me, meditation is the fast track to this connection. Performed under skillful guidance, through meditation, we reach points of internal union wherein the Truth of Self as an Eternal Spiritual Being becomes evident.

Along this journey of a thousand steps, we must also look inside to see what thoughts, ideas, and feelings we have buried within that prevent us from living a dynamic, creative, loving, and fulfilled life. Buddha called this the "First Turning of the Dharma Wheel," which means, we cannot become the beautiful, fulfilled, inspired people we are if we don't look to see what prevents us from being that Self.

Just as we can identify our Divine Spiritual Self through the Divine Aspects of Love, Wisdom, Beauty, Harmony, and Understanding, we must also identify the ego aspects that stand in the way of our Spiritual greatness. In Ro-Hun Therapy, we give these aspects a name: Negative Reactive Selves. They are as real, vital, and creative as our Divine Aspects. Our trouble comes when we don't recognize these Negative Reactive Selves as a part of us needing to be healed. We just say, "Well, that's me. Live with it."

No Negative Reactive Self ever led to fulfillment, joy, abundance, or love, so why would we want to claim it as who we are? The next chapter deals with these Negative Reactive Selves so that we can see their deadly destruction of our most beautiful life. Such a life is possible for everyone, but without guidance, help, and a deep desire to find it, we wander unfulfilled, frustrated, and deeply sad.

# CHAPTER 2

# *Negative Reactive Selves*

Now that we know we have a hidden place of buried pain and hurtful thoughts, we need to understand how these create havoc in our lives. These buried feelings and ideas have lives of their own, in a sense. Specific sets of circumstances trigger them into action, resulting in highly predictable and consistent chain reactions of negativity and negative behavior. These chain reactions are highly individualistic. An event that triggers one person might not trigger another. You might flare with anger in traffic while that bothers me not at all. I, however, could become angry when someone doesn't perform the way I think he or she should. As a result, we think we are different from each other, but the truth is, we all experience the same emotions in our own unique patterns. How my anger came to be born might not be how your anger was born. Anger, however, is anger. There are as many possible chain reactions and combinations as there are people. No matter what emotions we fall through when these chain reactions are activated, we fall, just as surely as if the floor opened beneath our feet and we plunged from one trap door through another.

One of my clients would immediately flare into anger when faced with opposition to one of his ideas. This reaction pushed people away, giving him physical, psychological, and emotional space. Yet this space, designed to keep him "safe," did just the opposite. Angry and alone, he dropped into personal doubt, and from doubt, he fell into confusion. But he didn't stop there. From confusion, he plunged into despair. He would sit in that cesspool sometimes for hours, paralyzed from taking action of any kind. He was, needless to say, confusing to his wife who, of course, was falling through her own trap doors. Nothing good ever came from this chain reaction, and ultimately, his wife left him, which is why he finally turned to Ro-Hun.

In pop psychology, these chain reactions are called "buttons" and they "are pushed." Well, they are more than buttons. They are living energies that can, and do, take over our lives whether or not we want them to *because we have given them the power to do so*. As we just saw with my client, they cause us to react without control, and they are devastating.

In Ro-Hun, we call these chain reactions Negative Reactive Selves. "Negative" because nothing good comes from them. "Reactive" because when we are caught in them, we cannot create a better solution. "Selves" because they behave the same way every time they are triggered, thereby seeming to have a life of their own. The results and our behavior are always predictable. We yell, or clam up, become aggressive or passive-aggressive, cry or whatever. Nothing ever changes. It cannot. We have given this part of ourselves the power to run our lives in those given circumstances. And where does that leave us? Usually, we don't feel good about ourselves. And where does *that* leave us?

There are a number of Negative Reactive Selves: the angry self, the blind self, the confused self, the blaming self, the controlling self, the frightened self, etc. They have more to them than just the emotional chain reaction, as we know. Each one also carries a very dangerous thought. In Ro-Hun, we call these "faulty thoughts," and the feelings are called "faulty feelings." "Faulty" means that the thoughts aren't of Truth. Negative emotions, therefore, are "faulty" because they don't permit us to express our Love, Wisdom, Harmony, Beauty, and Understanding. Our faulty thoughts and feelings, our Negative Reactive Selves, are the poison that pollutes the connection to our Higher Self and God daily. Ro-Hun is a *spiritual* process. The goal of Ro-Hun Therapy is to help us deepen, widen, and more clearly experience our connection with our Higher Self—that eternal Light of the Divine that is within every human who walks the face of the earth.

Truth is eternal; truth always exists. Reality comes and goes, according to our education, experience, and perception. When we have an injury, such as a cut finger, the reality is there is an injury, but having an injured finger isn't a truth because there will come a moment when that reality of an injured finger is no longer true. So, negative thoughts and feelings that run our lives from the cesspool are a reality because they do hurt us, but they aren't truth because they can be healed. The cesspool can be drained, and fresh, fertile, healthy thoughts and feelings can replace the old hurtful ones.

Remember my client who used anger to protect himself but then fell into despair? He had a series of damaging thoughts that went along with each of his emotions. First, in anger, he thought, "I am right and you are wrong." This led to self-righteousness, rigid thinking, and criticism of others. Then, when someone disagreed with him, he felt doubtful, and his thought was, "My ideas are no good," which is self-criticism and lack of trust. Following that, he felt confusion and this thought lead to, "What are the right ideas?" This process led him to giving away personal power. He ended up in despair with the thought, "I have nothing to offer," which froze him into inactivity and paralysis. While these thoughts and feelings were his particular choices, they might not be someone else's choices. His Angry Self said, "I am right and you are wrong." Another person's

Angry Self might say, "No one ever hears me," while someone else might have the thought, "I have to use anger to get what I want." Whatever the thoughts, they aren't good and don't do anything to promote healthy self-esteem, good relationships, or happiness. Ultimately, we struggle away from the feelings and thoughts by driving them once more back into the cesspool where they remain. Until the next trigger occurs.

Ro-Hun powerfully and directly addresses Negative Reactive Selves and the pain they cause. Guided by the therapist, clients become sensitive to the energy and emotion of whatever has been buried. They are encouraged to make connections between their feelings and their life events. As the clients respond, the therapist guides them further until they discover each Negative Reactive Self. The faulty thoughts and feelings are identified and refined, until the client has an "a-ha" moment of clarity and understanding of the various Selves and the resulting damage to their lives. Then, clients are able to understand how they themselves have created their lives through the Negative Reactive Selves. This is pure discovery with very little input from the therapist except to guide and help refine through skillful questioning. The triumph for each client, then, becomes very personal, powerful, and cleansing.

Of course, these sessions are quite emotional. We cannot heal what we cannot feel, so connecting with the emotions of the Negative Reactive Selves and the damage done in our lives is absolutely necessary. No one ever died because he or she identified and felt a buried feeling. People have become ill, however, because they *haven't* identified and healed negative feelings. Repressed feelings, both positive and negative, affect your immune system as well as your internal chemistry (read *Molecules of Emotion* by Dr. Candace Pert). Who hasn't heard of stress-induced ulcers and heart attacks? Who hasn't heard cancer called the anger disease? This connection between mind and body makes finding and healing those Negative Reactive Selves even more imperative.

It is quite sobering to realize how much of life has been created through the Negative Reactive Selves. However, we also have within us the beautiful antidote to these poisonous, subversive thoughts and feelings. That antidote, that healing grace, is our Spirit, and the power of our Spirit enables us to move in amazing and miraculous ways, releasing us from the bondage of ignorance and repetitive failure.

# CHAPTER 3

## *The Power of Spirit*

Ro-Hun is a spiritually based therapy, which makes it work so powerfully. All healing comes from our Spiritual Selves. We are truly spiritual beings who are having physical experiences. Countless books have been written about our involution as Souls to earth and our evolution back Home. Here is a version shortened to be more understandable and less dogmatic.

Long before we had a body, we were a Soul, a Spiritual Individual. We lived, expressed, and created from our spiritual qualities of Love, Harmony, Wisdom, Beauty, and Understanding. We were Beings of Light lacking the density of matter, living in peace and love without competition or stress or striving. Some religions call this state of being Heaven. I call it a state of Oneness.

Then, we were born into physical bodies. It was a dramatic change of state. In Oneness, every soul was in perfect harmony with one another and The Divine Creator. Every thought and feeling was open to everyone else. Nothing was, or could be, hidden. Nothing needed to be. Once we were born into bodies, we transitioned into a state of diversity where our true nature was essentially hidden or masked in our physical bodies. Suddenly, we felt separated and alone, scared and isolated. When we live in fear and separation, the opposites of Love and Oneness are created from fear and separation.

Hello, Grave of Buried Feelings! Hello, birth of Negative Reactive Selves!

Because our natural Self is one of Light and Love, the source of all healing, Ro-Hun must take us back there to remember who we are in order to reclaim our power. This is quite different from other forms of emotional/mental therapy, which rely on an exploration of our psychological selves only. In Ro-Hun, a spiritual connection is vital for healing to happen. No one will surrender any part of himself or herself, no matter how painful, if there isn't some other part that feels better, *and they can go there at will.*

Further, the mind and emotions that are part of the problem are—without connection to our Higher Self—our only sources of help! How can the wounded inner child help the wounded inner child heal? When we are connected to our Higher Self, we have a deep, powerful resource of Love, Wisdom, Harmony, Beauty, and Understanding to pull from. Therefore, every Ro-Hun session begins with a process of reconnecting with the Spiritual Self. It is only from that place of clarity, where we can feel the spiritual truth about who we are, that we have the strength and motivation to take a look at all the Negative Reactive Selves tucked away in the Grave of Buried Feelings. From this spiritual reconnection, we have a personal, real, and direct experience of our Self as a Being of Light. Direct experience like this is a great gift because once we have made that connection, we can never again be as lost as we once were; we can never again be as hurt as we were. Knowing who we are, we are empowered to open that Grave of Buried Feelings and let all the poisonous Negative Reactive Selves out, one by one, to the light of day and the Light of God. That's spiritual. That's healing. That's powerful.

When I tell prospective clients that we are going to perform this kind of spiritual reconnection, I am frequently met with doubtful stares. After all, they have come for therapy because their lives are falling apart. They aren't sure they can find anything good inside of themselves. What makes me so confident that connection can be made? I know we can make that connection because the Soul is calling the client home. When someone says, "Yes, I want Ro-Hun," I know the soul is calling because Ro-Hun is such a spiritually connected process. Because our basic nature is spiritual, everything is in place to take a client to their own space of power, love, and wisdom because that's who they really are.

A Ro-Hun therapist, therefore, sees a client as a whole, beautiful, radiant being, who has temporarily lost his or her way in the morass of a difficult world. We see and relate to the client's wholeness, not the issues or problems that cause separation from that wholeness. Because a Ro-Hun therapist *knows* their client is already healthy, they are able to move the client towards that health in a process and progression that brings the client back into his or her own natural healthy state.

Another reason that Ro-Hun is so effective is that it doesn't become stuck on the stories that are the repository of the client's issues. Negative Reactive Selves are born from events that become our personal stories. Of course, an unresolved Negative Reactive Self keeps cropping up repeatedly. In Ro-Hun, we find the story, a life event, but we don't remain on the story. The story—frozen in place in the consciousness—is the structure through which the Negative Reactive Selves (issues) continually wreak havoc.

For example, here is a story:

*My father came home every night drunk and beat up my mother. I had to watch because later it was my turn to be hit.*

This painful story could result in any of one of several Negative Reactive Selves (issues), such as:

*Untrusting Self: I can't trust men/women/children/teachers/ God (you name it). I feel alone.*
*Controlling Self: I have to control everything or things will fall apart. I feel afraid.*
*Helpless Self: I am weak and helpless. I feel like nothing.*
*Unlovable Self: No one can love me. I feel defective.*
*Unimportant Self: I don't matter. I feel invisible.*

(Note that these are not the only possible combinations of thoughts and feelings for the Selves for this story, only examples.)

Therapeutically, we must talk about the story because that starts the emotional connections flowing. But we cannot remain talking about the story because no resolution will come. The Negative Reactive Self born from the event carries the seeds of the issue with its faulty thoughts and feelings. Without moving forward into discovering the faulty thoughts and feelings, the client becomes caught in the "blame game" resulting from the story.

*If he hadn't done that...*
*If she hadn't stood there...*
*If I had stopped him...*

Blame is an endless, repetitive, and unproductive behavior; no true healing, resolution, or forgiveness comes from blame. In Ro-Hun, we move past blame into understanding and then forgiveness—two key ingredients in healing. With healing, we can examine our lives and see how the faulty thoughts and feelings from one bad situation repeated themselves. Now, we are in positions to make a real change through new choices.

Our beautiful qualities of Wisdom, Love, Beauty, Harmony, and Understanding have been covered by stories and negative thoughts and feelings in layers, like an onion. Going directly to the core of all that pain would be a terrifying experience in just one leap. Ro-Hun peels away the layers, one by one, at one's own individual pace and depth. Some of the stories we remember, and some we have buried so deeply that they have been forgotten. It is truly magical when old, buried, and completely forgotten stories rise to the surface, and the hidden secret pain is released. Whether we know the story or discover it for the first time, the result is freedom to express our most beautiful and creative and loving selves in our lives.

Invariably, clients look physically different when a session is concluded. More light is in their faces and eyes, and sometimes the very contours of their faces change. Often they say, "The pressure is gone." All the internal pressure from the faulty thoughts and feelings is carried as physical pressure—back, stomach, head, and neck—as if it is the client's natural state. People have learned to live with the most awful physical pain and pressure, and their astonishment when it is relieved is amazing. That's the power of faulty thoughts and feelings. They make you think that discomfort, pressure, pain, physical inconvenience, and even physical illness is a natural part of life. It doesn't have to be. Of course we age and bodies change, but we don't have to live with pain caused by our Negative Reactive Selves. As we heal through this dynamic process, a kind of alchemical reaction takes place. Out of the quagmire of our pain and suffering, a new life dawns physically, mentally, emotionally, and spiritually, as surely as the sun rises each morning.

# PART ONE: TWO STEPS TO FORGIVENESS

‿ා෴

# Purification
# and
# The Caged One

‿ා෴

*"We cannot change anything unless we accept it.*
*There can be no transforming of darkness into light and apathy*
*into movement without emotion."*
—C. G. Jung

# CHAPTER 4

## *Purification*

There are many layers to self-awareness. These layers are, in effect, points of view through which we experience ourselves and our environments, our pasts and our presents. For example, humans have, to greater or lesser degrees, Angry Selves. To heal and balance, we must address our Angry Selves from various points of view in order to understand their scope and effects. One point of view is that the Angry Self is a Victim. Another is the Angry Self as a Control Method. Still another point of view or layer of awareness is the Angry Self as Self-hatred Sabotage. Each layer discovered brings deeper and deeper healing to the Angry Self. Therefore, to discover these layers, Ro-Hun takes you through several processes, each one building on the insights and understandings of the one before so that the journey into one's innermost faulty thoughts and negative feelings is an organized, rational one. Each process has a specific set of goals, and they are performed in an intentional order, designed to help the client heal in a healthy, sustainable manner. If we heal our consciousness, our awareness, from the top down, so to speak, we will be healing in the aforementioned organized and rational way. It is much like chopping down a big tree. First, you top the tree, then you cut out section by section until finally you can dig out the roots. We are built, consciously speaking, in much the same way. The roots of our fears and angers are buried deeply and not accessed easily, unless we have done some recognizing and healing first.

The first Ro-Hun process is called Purification. It's a big name for a big process because it deals with the Victim Self. To prepare for such deep work, clients need to feel the powerful truth of who they really are. They are not the hurt person who is seeking therapy. They are more than just their pain. They are beautiful, wise, loving Souls who have become caught up in the difficulties of physical life and drawn into the Grave of Buried Feelings. During the Purification Induction, the very first experience of Ro-Hun, clients are gently led into an encounter with themselves as Love, Wisdom, and Harmony, three of their Spiritual Aspects. This is quite possibly their first experience with their Spiritual Aspects. It can be mind blowing. This is a powerful, life-altering experience because when we feel that kind of love, there is no denying its existence. No one is the same after that. Spiritual connection and the resulting loving empowerment are what enable us to take the plunge into the Grave of Buried Feelings. Without our spiritual strength, we are often tempted to give up hoping or trying for a better life and push on with the Grave of Buried Feelings fully intact, reacting and creating problems.

Purification is all about forgiveness. People have hurt us, disappointed us, and abused us. We must forgive them; there is no way around that stone in the heart. Forgiveness doesn't mean that what they did was okay; it means that we choose to stop being victimized by the memories and the pain associated with them. Lack of forgiveness is like nailing one foot to the floor. We want to move forward, but the old situations keep us captive in emotional circles and damaging experiences. Forgiveness through Purification is a powerful choice toward personal freedom and healing.

In every situation, happy or unhappy, we make conclusions about ourselves. If the situation is a happy one, our conclusions are that we are loving, generous, talented, a good person, etc. If the situation isn't a happy one, we make other conclusions, such as deciding we are invisible, weak, unlovable, and so forth. These are the feelings that become stuffed in the grave because we don't want to feel them, and we certainly don't want to tell anyone else that we feel them. Purification brings us to the grave and hands us the shovel. Purification addresses these emotional traps directly. Not only does Purification hand us the power to expose, heal, and cleanse those Negative Reactive Selves, it teaches us how to excavate, how to approach what we find, and how to bring those sorrowful feelings to the Light of God for healing. Ro-Hun is actually a blueprint for living because it teaches us the loving way to heal our pain—and Love IS the healer.

One of my clients, Alan, was a man caught in rage. It erupted with regularity and was aimed mostly at his family, but also at other drivers when he was behind the wheel of a car. According to Alan, his wife and children could not do anything right, and he feared they would hurt themselves through their inabilities to manage life. As years went on, the rage grew until his family could barely tolerate him. He admitted to me, even before we began the therapeutic work, that he realized he was filled with rage and quite ashamed of his uncontrollable outbursts. "They don't know," he said to me vehemently, "what can happen if they aren't on the alert. Someone has to pay attention." That "someone" was him, and his family resented him greatly for his ever-watchful, critical eye.

During his first session of Purification, the cause came bubbling out and he wept profusely at the memory. When he was young, five or six years of age, he parents gave him a dog, and he proudly cared for the little animal, making certain that water was always available and that it was fed regularly. He was also responsible for letting the dog go outside when necessary. One winter morning, he let the dog out and then became distracted by something his younger brother was doing. His father left for work, allowing the storm door to slam shut. The sound of the slamming door made Alan think of his dog outside. As he stood at the storm door, he watched in horror as his father backed the car down the driveway toward the dog. Alan began screaming, "Stop! Stop! Stop!" Caught as he was in his little boy terror, he could not get the storm door opened. He saw the car crush the dog.

During all the intervening years, from age five or six to his mature age of 50, that experience had been buried deeply within him until that moment in therapy. While the event was unimaginable, the buried pain was huge. He'd been speaking that pain all these years. We ultimately discerned his thoughts and feelings:

*Thought: I have to be constantly on vigil.*
*Feelings: helpless, fearful*
*Thought: I can't trust anybody.*
*Feelings: isolated and angry*
*Thought: Life can be eradicated if I don't pay attention.*
*Feelings: powerless, responsible, and angry*

Buried patterns like Alan's are inside all of us. Perhaps they are not as dramatically authored, but they are painful nevertheless. Imagine that you discover, in your Grave of Buried Feelings, a particular set of beliefs that runs something like this:

*Thought: I am so different no one really understands me.*
*Feeling: despair*
*Thought: Love is everywhere, but not for me.*
*Feeling: unworthy*
*Thought: I have to work very hard and be frugal.*

*Feelings: emptiness and lack*
*Thought: No one appreciates my knowledge and me.*
*Feeling: invisibility*
*Thought: I wish I had someone strong in my life to guide me.*
*Feelings: weak, helpless, and indecisive*
*Thought: I can't trust people.*
*Feeling: betrayal*

Imagine that these feelings create a set of eyeglasses that you wear daily. With those eyeglasses, you can only see despair, unworthiness, emptiness, lack, invisibility, weakness, helplessness, and indecisiveness. Because those feelings and thoughts are what you believe to be true, you will attract to you people and situations that prove your beliefs. Then, because our experiences prove to us over and over who we are, we assume that this is life.

Naturally, you also have good feelings. You have felt strong, smart, or beautiful, and you have taken on positive thoughts, but the grave and those buried feelings are constantly pulling you away from holding on to the good feelings. You know that's true. One day, you feel on top of the world, and the next you don't. Why? You can say it's because of so-and-so or a world event or politics or whatever, but the truth is that you have fallen into that grave and are seeing the world through those hidden beliefs. It doesn't take much to fall there because we know these beliefs are the truth about us since they appear to prove themselves over and over. The names, dates, and places in your life story might change, but if you go through your life wearing the same set of beliefs, the people cannot be essentially different, nor can your experiences be any different.

We've all heard that women marry their fathers and men marry their mothers or that a second marriage often imitates the first. Now, we can see why. If we do not change our inner vision of ourselves, we are destined to repeat the patterns. Without healing them, there is nothing else to do. Healing, then, helps us change how we see ourselves. Once we change the author of our life stories, we change the stories.

If you feel you are so different that no one can understand you, then you can only experience the sadness of never feeling a sense of belonging or oneness. A shared life is not one you can have. You feel loneliness, even if you are married or part of a huge family. All you will perceive is your difference and your separation. Ro-Hun helps you find this feeling of despair and the thought that goes with it, "I am so different no one really understands me." The therapist leads you to understand the circumstances that happened when you decided to take on this thought and feeling and then guides you to forgive the Negative Reactive Self that was born during that difficult time and to forgive the people who "caused" you to feel this way. I put "caused" in quotes because no one made you choose your feelings of isolation and despair. That was your power to decide what you would believe of yourself, and you were the one who selected, out of an entire range of possible feelings, exactly which feeling you would hold. And hold. And live with.

It is amazing to feel and watch as a client suddenly begins to connect the dots. Awareness dawns like a new day as he or she realizes how his or her very own thoughts and feelings created havoc with his or her life over and over. It is such a freeing moment because the client *never has to do it again*. That is the wonder of Ro-Hun. In an instant, you are free to choose new responses, new thoughts, and a new set of beliefs once you understand the patterns and have forgiven everyone involved. It is such a powerful moment when that unhappy part of self heals. Relief fills the room with Light.

When revisiting hurtful situations, one question always comes up: "How could they do that to me?" This is a necessary question to understand because understanding brings healing as well as forgiveness. In fact, understanding precedes forgiveness. While it is true that you cannot heal what you do not feel, you can neither release nor embrace what you do not understand. The cognitive mind needs understanding; otherwise, it will wonder and question and divert you from your healing, always asking, "why?" Through Ro-Hun, you will be able to revisit your painful story and, this time, see exactly why the people in your life did what they did to you. Your therapist helps you to see your perpetrator's reasons for hurting you, and the reasons don't have anything to do with you at all.

Let's look at the painful story we used in the last chapter:

*My father came home every night drunk and beat up my mother. I had to watch because later it was my turn to be hit.*

After identifying the thoughts and feelings you took on from that story—for example, "I am weak," and the feeling of help-lessness—your therapist will help you take a deeper look at your father than you have ever taken before. Invariably, you find that your father hurt and abused you and your mother not because he hated you both, but because he felt weak himself, or insecure, or unimportant, or frightened of life, or any number of debilitating feelings. Maybe he was abused, and his idea of relationships was one of pain and domination. You will be able to see the pain, abuse, and trouble he lived through, which made him who and what he is. This insight, this understanding leads to forgiveness—the key to all healing. It also leads you into Wisdom and out of being a victim. Truth is our map, Love is our strength, and Wisdom is our guide.

For every thought, there is a feeling; for every feeling, there is a thought. A thought and feeling combined and used repeatedly creates a Negative Reactive Self. This consistent use of hurtful patterns creates an actual rut, or ditch, in your energy field, making the pattern easier and easier to fall into until you don't even realize you are living a pattern. One by one, your therapist leads you to discover your Negative Reactive Selves. One by one, the Negative Reactive Selves are found, heard, understood, loved, and healed.

With Purification, you have taken shovel in hand and opened the Grave of Buried Feelings. You have brought into the light of day the feelings you intuitively or actually knew you had but didn't have any idea how to handle them. The vault has been breached! Time for celebration!

Enjoy the fruits of your labors. Enjoy the peace, release, and relaxation that you haven't felt for a long time. Savor the results and relish the moment. You have established a new and healthier relationship with yourself and with those around you. Recognize what you have accomplished. It is just as important to recognize your growth as it is necessary to open that grave.

After your three Purification sessions, you will go about your life in a stronger state. The world will look clearer and you feel the freedom of all the releasing you accomplished. Notice your changes, both subtle and not so subtle. You'll find yourself responding to your life in new and different ways. Most importantly, you will feel different about yourself—calmer, more focused, far less reactive, and with greater emotional balance. Maybe your family and friends will notice; they often do. Maybe you will be the one noticing your changes. In both cases, inhale and feel good. Take deep breaths when you feel your newness, when you respond instead of react, when you behave more positively and good new experiences come your way. If you take a small moment and inhale deeply, feeling and recognizing what has transpired, you will be drawing your healing into yourself even more deeply and in a very conscious way. Deep breathing is a wonderful way to maintain your sense of healing and clarity.

This state of newness will last for a period of time that varies for each client. At any rate, you will feel good and should enjoy those feelings. Eventually, however, other Negative Reactive Selves that could not be accessed during Purification will make themselves known through their sad, victim-like feelings. That's because once the Grave of Buried Feelings has been opened, all the poisonous thoughts and feelings begin to seek the Light; they naturally bubble up. You might experience short bouts of sadness or feeling lost, or you might find yourself in a lethargy that is new, or a host of relatively minor disturbances will arise to disturb your newfound healing.

This means that all is progressing as it should and you are ready for a Skim.

A Skim is a single session that addresses these newly emerging Negative Reactive Selves and clears them out. Think of it as a "mopping up" operation. Some people need several Skim sessions; others do not. In either case, as you share with your therapist what you are experiencing in your life, he or she will guide you as necessary until you are ready to heal the next layer called, the Caged One.

CHAPTER 5

# The Caged One

 

Through Purification, you addressed your Victim Self. You identified the thoughts about yourself that you took on from your painful experiences, and you forgave those involved. That step alone is a major turning point. Following Purification, you are able to hear the voice of the Victim all around you, on television, at the water cooler, on the golf course. Blame is a natural part of the human experience, one we must experience and grow past. You have seen directly what very few people have seen. You are a creator because now you are able to consciously, and with love, choose your responses and change your thoughts. No longer are you the eternal Victim of others! That's what gives you a beautiful high feeling following Purification; you are able to make choices you could not make before. However, as you do the Skims your therapist suggests, the next level gradually begins to make itself known. When that happens, you aren't feeling so high and good.

Suddenly, occurrences that are usually small irritations take on larger proportions. You might awaken one morning to find yourself surrounded by idiots. Life begins to cave in. The feelings you feel are much worse than the sad, lost victim feelings of Purification. Anger often rises with a new vengeance, and it seems the world conspires to block you at every turn. You wonder just what you did all that work for—and what the therapist missed—because you are feeling miserable. Nothing goes well, and all the good feelings you felt from your therapy disappear like smoke in the wind. Ro-Hun didn't work. You are convinced of it. If it had, why are you so miserable?

The truth is that Ro-Hun worked quite well. Because you successfully healed in the Purification process and eliminated the protective layer of victimization, you have exposed the layer of the Caged One. The Caged One, the next layer of that Grave of Buried Feelings, is beginning to rise, and it is mad! It wants you to return, and it is working on you from its dank lair to pull you away from good feelings because it cannot survive on good feelings. It needs your fear, anger, and misery. When you explore and heal the Caged One, you release yourself from being the eternal victim of ... *yourself!* But first, one must understand what the Caged One looks like.

Inside each of us is the Shadow or Dark Side. You can't escape from it. Everyone—the preacher in the pulpit, the saint in the ghetto, the inspired leader, the meditating yogi, the bank robber, the rapist, and the murderer—has a dark side. The dark side is just more evident in those who carry out dark deeds. It's part of the deal here in the world of matter. This world is full of opposites and opposing forces that create havoc and destruction in lives. This destructive force is called the Caged One or the Abuser.

Now that the protective layer of victimization has been removed through Purification, we are able to identify the voice of the Caged One. It whispers lies to us that we believe, such as:

*No one can love you.*
*There is no God.*
*Life is tough and then you die.*
*There is no love.*
*Life is a joke.*
*You are all alone.*

Who is speaking? Who would put such evil, destructive thoughts in our minds and hearts? Just as there is a God, there is a "Not-God," who is also powerful but in a different way than God is. The Not-God is powerful because it rules through fear and intimidation. It does not possess the Love, Wisdom, and Harmony of God, yet it knows you very, very well. It knows all your weaknesses, fears, hesitations, and doubts, and it preys on all of them. In religions, this Not-God has many names, including Satan, Devil, Ahriman, and Loki, but they all refer to the same thing. In Ro-Hun, we call the Not-God the Trickster because it does just that. It tricks you, fools you, pulls you in, and holds you captive believing the lies and negativity that it creates.

Does this mean an external being goes around infecting us with evil? Not at all. Just as God is within us all, so is the Not-God. We have the idea of God, and if we pursue that idea, we discover that, indeed, God is real and within us. If we pursue the idea of Not-God or Trickster, we will find it alive inside us as well. The Trickster is actually easier to find because we are ruled by it more than by God, believing as we do in the lies that the Trickster whispers in our ears.

Ro-Hun guides you in discovering the Truth about yourself, that you are Light and Wisdom and Love and Harmony. The Trickster cannot tolerate you knowing who you are, and so the darkness works harder to pull you back from your spiritual strength. Every time you find a spiritual strength, attribute, or ability the Trickster will pull harder. It has to. It is fighting for its life, and your energy is the only life it has. Every time you heal a Negative Reactive Self, you diminish the power of the Trickster, and the Trickster cannot permit that to happen.

Unlike Negative Reactive Selves, focused in their pain, the Trickster openly creates doubt and fear in *you*. Therefore, you must face the Trickster itself. Your therapst guides you gently into the darkness until you approach the Trickster's lair. The Trickster presents itself in many forms. Some forms are frightening to call forth your fear, such as huge snakes or viscious faces. Or, it may come as a crying baby, cowering woman or helpless man to prey on your compassion. The Trickster uses every way it can to keep you ensnared in darkness and lies. And it is not afraid of you. At all. It doesn't believe you have the ability to unseat it from its unholy throne. Yet, through Ro-Hun, that's exactly what you can, and will, do. One by one, you face the lies you have believed about yourself, love, God, and goodness, and you heal them. Because you removed the veil of the Victim through Purification, you are able to stand in Light and defeat this Prince of Darkness.

We call this process the Caged One because you have done just that—caged these horrible thoughts and feelings so that you won't be aware of them. They are there nonetheless in the second layer of that Grave of Buried Feelings, spewing poison and decay from the cesspool into your consciousness. No one wants to admit or recognize that we really do "know" that *we are unlovable*. But if that is one of your Caged ideas, you really do believe it.

What would that dark belief of *"I am unlovable"* sound like or look like to others? Perhaps you find yourself saying, "There are no good men or women out there." That statement could surely come from knowing you are unlovable. You could never find the right person for you because you *know it can't happen*. Your friends will commiserate with you, acknowledge that there aren't any good ones anymore, and everyone goes on about their business. The fact is, your belief is what is operating in you, and you can continue to forever look for and never find anyone with whom to share a loving relationship because it remains impossible. Even if you did find someone, the relationship would eventually crumble because of your underlying belief that you are unlovable.

Another possibility is that you will make yourself unapproachable in some way. Have you ever known anyone brash, loud, and unrefined, whose very utterances are grating? Perhaps that person is feeling unlovable and has to push others away to prove it. Conversely, this belief could create a hermit who just won't try. Or it could force someone into the public eye, searching for love and recognition. There are a thousand ways that one thought could manifest itself so that, on the surface, no one can see what is going on. It's all Caged. It's the underbelly of the iceberg. That's the destructive power of the Trickster.

There is another, terrible aspect of the Caged thoughts and feelings. Even as you are hurting yourself (these are *your* thoughts and feelings) and permitting these poisons to affect your life, *you will also abuse others*. The awful truth is, through the Trickster, every single one of us is an abuser, a perpetrator of pain and suffering. No one wants to hear or acknowledge the fact, but the truth remains, just as you abuse yourself, you abuse others.

When you are convinced that you cannot be loved, you make certain others know they are not lovable. You cut them down somehow, some way, either directly or in a passive-aggressive manner. It doesn't take much to make others feel unlovable. For example, a dismissive gesture, a snide look, an under-handed comment, or a slight laugh can do just that. A never-ending flow of criticism or constant pressure on others to do things your way can convince them they are unloved. Then there is always the direct approach, actually telling the people in your life how unattractive, useless, or dumb they are. Whatever your style, however you abuse yourself, you also abuse others. You are not inherently mean, but when you are caught in the darkness within, you cannot share anything other than darkness. What is inner becomes outer.

After Purification, therefore, you *must* go through the Caged

One process. Otherwise, all those lies that fill your mind from this dark inner space will undermine, erode, and destroy the work of Purification. Once you understand and face the Trickster, you won't be fooled. You'll know that when life falls apart, you are ready to catch the Trickster at its game. You will grab the shovel once more and, with all your might, dig deeper with greater determination to be free.

# CHAPTER 6

## *Deepening Spiritual Strength*

What a ride! Through the Purification Process, you healed your Victim Self, and through the Caged One Process, you pulled the mask from your Abusive Self. When you look at what you have accomplished and see how far you have come, you will be so proud! You have learned how to take ownership of your life circumstances; you have learned to forgive, and you have bravely faced denial and lies. Even more importantly, you have experienced yourself as a Spiritual being of Light, Wisdom, Love and Harmony. It is your Spiritual Self, your Soul, that has provided the depth and perception that have empowered you to address what lies beneath the surface of your awareness. Knowing you are so much more than whatever is in that Grave of Buried Feelings enables you to look at yourself deeply and honestly. This Light is the absolute author of your life. However, it cannot create with all the goodness and plenty it has to offer because you are not fully aware of it, nor can you be until you reach the very core of the self-deceptions and personal lies you hold. Even though you have accomplished much, more remains in the Grave of Buried Feelings to excavate, more is left to release and transform into Truth.

By now, you have become quite excited about yourself and your prospects. You are feeling the difference in your life and seeing the results of your inner work in your relationships and life experiences. Frequently, at this point, therapists begin to hear clients using words like "magic" and "amazing" and phrases like, "I can't believe it." Magically, a thorny problem at work dissolves. Amazingly, a spouse who seemed distant will soften. Money has been known to show up, doors have opened, and solutions have been discovered without the usual stress. Your motivation strengthens because you discover that you would rather have the honey of life than the vinegar. You are eager to continue.

Unlike Purification and the Caged One, which must proceed in progressive order, the next four Ro-Hun processes—Origin, Divine Mother, Androgynous, and Seven Visions of Self—can be experienced in any order. Through them, you continue to explore the depth of the faulty thoughts and feelings that you've been carrying around inside of you. Not only are you releasing more of the poison, but also, you are building your Light and strengthening your connection with your Soul. You are becoming freer to experience the wonderful truth of yourself as a Spiritual being living a physical life. Life begins to take on a different perspective with a more beautiful hue of vitality and vibrancy. As you feel more alive, real, and present, you become more skilled at living your life and more excited by the possibilities. We will look at each of the next four processes in the next section. Here, I'd like to recap where you've been and give you some understanding of the relationship between your Soul and your personality (ego).

In the beginning of Ro-Hun, clients are often fearful of revealing the less-than-perfect side of themselves. This is natural. We don't want others to know that we are insecure and scared, that we feel phoney, and if they only knew how weak we were, they would roll over us like a freight train. We don't want people to know that we are riddled with self-doubt and that we try very hard to be accepted. By the time you finish the Caged One, you begin to lose that awful, useless, self-protective attitude, and you become more willing to find, feel, and live with even greater freedom. Now that you have forgiven others and yourself, the first major step in any healing, you are clear enough to see more of the untruths you have used to *keep yourself bound and captive.*

As if becoming free from your own Grave of Buried Feelings isn't enough, bringing peace and healing to your life, Ro-Hun is also a *way* of life. Through Ro-Hun, you learn how to work with difficulties as they arise, and they will, of course. Buddha told us that life is a series of vicissitudes and troubles will be around us always. It's the nature of life. Jobs will fail, and people will leave through choice or death; bills have to be paid regardless of fluctuating finances; health can become uncertain or compromised. Ro-Hun teaches us how to address the faulty thoughts and feelings that arise because of life's circumstances. We are able to be our own healer. Now, that's exciting!

Further, you learn through uncovering the Negative Reactive Selves that you are a Divine Creator and a Creator always creates. As a result, whether you are creating chaos from fear or peace from love, you are the one who has made your life what it is through your choices of which thoughts and feelings you would hold. Until you are free from the blame game—they/she/he did this and that to me—you will always be the victim of others. When you realize your ability to create the life you want, you discover a major Truth about how life really works.

Understanding the relationship between Soul and personality is necessary. The personality—the ways you express yourself throughout your life—is part of you that is caught up in your faulty thoughts and feelings. Of course, you have positive thoughts and feelings as well, but the unhappy ones, as we have seen, hurt you. The personality is another name for the ego. Sometimes the ego is called the "little i" and it is expressed through the personality.

Beyond the personality is our Soul, the "I Am," and the Divine Person who we are. Our Soul's task on earth is to express itself here, to manifest its Divine qualities of Love, Wisdom, Harmony, and Beauty. The ego, however, is caught in its fears and self-doubt and stands in the way. It's like the sun and fog. When the fog (the ego) rolls in, the warm, life-giving energy of the sun (the Soul) cannot be seen or felt. When we are in the fog, we are disoriented, we cannot see where we are going, and we become fearful because nothing is clear to us. We do many things—make plans and goals—but following them is often difficult, and we lose our way. Ultimately, when the ego becomes aware of the Soul, the warmth and life of the Soul, the sun, is clearly present. The sun has always been there, even when the fog seemed so dense and permanent. When the sun shines through, when the Soul emerges from the fog of the ego, life takes on a new glow and a new health, and that glow and health spread to others.

The completion of the Purification and the Caged One processes creates within you a momentous movement toward clarity; they part the fog, but only briefly. The inner strength and knowledge necessary to keep the fog at bay must continue to be developed. We have to peel back each layer and continue to address the faulty thoughts and feelings systematically until we have established mastery of ourselves. The Purification and the Caged One processes alone do not pull out the roots. To reach the place where you have the clarity of self and personal spiritual strength to tackle the roots, you must first build your strength of Light through the four processes of Origin, Divine Mother, Androgynous, and Seven Visions of Self. Together, your therapist and you will determine exactly which process is right for you to begin with and the order in which you perform the others. It really depends on the events in your life because your experiences and conditions dictate what needs to be done. These incredibly beautiful and enlightening processes lead you forward, providing a deep, rich, and powerful inner platform on which you can stand. Through these processes, your trust in yourself as well as your ability to create from Light expand and bring you back into the wholeness and personal unity that are yours by birthright.

# PART TWO: BUILDING LIGHT

❦

## The Origin
## The Divine Mother
## The Androgynous
## The Seven Visions of Self

❦

*One does not become enlightened by imaging figures of light, but by making the darkness conscious.*
*—C.G. Jung*

# CHAPTER 7

## *The Origin*

Prior to entering the physical realm, all was in Oneness. Think of that time as a vast ocean. That ocean represents God, which depicts the concept of Oneness. All parts of the ocean's water are the same, which is to say, undifferentiated. As drops of water in that great ocean, we all bear the same properties as each other, but we cannot be cognizant of each as separate beings because we aren't. There is no "me" or "you" or "us". Entering the physical world of matter and duality, we separated from our Creator, and then our energy was forced to divide into male and female. Naked and alone in physical bodies, we had to survive in an environment that was new to us, and we embraced some very interesting beliefs about God and ourselves. To borrow the title of a book written long ago, we were *Strangers in a Strange Land*. We were disoriented and uncertain. The clarity we possessed when in Oneness was gone. Instead, we learned to defend ourselves, to be wary of each other, and to rely on our own strengths to survive. In the midst of all the turmoil, we had to seek each other out to procreate, forming larger tribes than those in the neighboring lands so that we could survive their onslaught or overwhelm them with our numbers. Sex and the need to procreate pulled us together, but there wasn't much love, wisdom, beauty, or harmony. Instead, there was much separation, fear, and defense.

Our focus was on survival, but beneath our needs, we were

confused. We intuitively remembered where we had come from. So, how did we end up here? Alone. Scared. Confused. This simplifies a long, complex process, but basically, at the core of us most of us believe that God either didn't like us or that we had done something horrendous. In either case, we were ousted from paradise. Because of this, we carry a burden of unworthiness, and this unworthiness is what the Caged One preyed upon, expanded, and turned into an art form, trapping us in cycles of despair, self-doubt, loss, and abandonment. Unworthiness keeps us separated from each other and from God.

You know what goes on inside of you when you meet people with whom you feel inferior. Even when you attempt conversation and interaction, you feel as if you are standing apart, and you don't belong, knowing that you are different and unacceptable in some way. You wonder if your clothes are right, or if your hair looks good, or if you should have lost those few extra pounds. You wish you had been more intelligent or witty. If you had done the correct things, you'd fit in. Right? Even if you do all these things, do those feelings go away? No. They are just buried deeper. This unworthiness comes from our original feelings of separation from God. God is somewhere out there, at worst, judging us and, at best, ignoring us.

In fact, this separation from God has a purpose. Just as a child pushes the boundaries with his or her parents and tries to establish his or her separate self, we too must separate from our Parent in order to become fully functioning, complete human beings. Yet this very separation from God prevents us from creating a full and flowing relationship with the Divine because we believe the separation is our fault. It is a catch-22. We need the separation to grow up, yet because of separation, we resent God and are not free to develop fully.

In Oneness, there is no male or female. Only One. The first

part of Creation, then, separated us into male and female. God Itself is male and female flowing in a united Oneness. As we were formed, that Oneness separated into the two energies of male and female. So let's imagine a Spiritual Male and a Spiritual Female in the mythical Garden of Eden. While they appear to be separate, they remain joined energetically, not physically. This is the Soul preparing to enter earth. Male energy is our outward dynamic energy. All actions, accomplishment, and doing are male. Female energy is our inward receptive energy. All reflection, inspiration, insight, and learning are female.

To illustrate, here is a story: The male and female, halves of the same whole but now in separate forms, are distinct and apart from each other and their Parent (God), for the first time. This causes a few ripples of concern. It is all very new and a bit bewildering. Then comes the final act of bewilderment—the creation into the physical world of matter. Once the soul is in physical matter, it loses all sense of direction and all sense of self. It is an astonishing thing to be invested in a physical body of the densest matter. Before, with God, it was all Love and Wisdom, Joy and Harmony, but in the physical world, there is confusion, the birth of fear and anger, and many decisions that aren't helpful: "I'll have to stay in my power to be safe." "I'll have to cling to someone else in order to be safe," and others. Off we go on our long, long journey back to remembering the truth of who we are. Among the feelings is anger toward God. We end up feeling very less-than and unworthy. Guilt reigns.

The Origin Process explores your earliest thoughts and feelings taken on when you found yourself out of paradise and on the earth. You discover the fear, anger, and resentment your own male and female energies took on. Imagine it. You were helpless in a new world made of hardened matter and filled with the impression of separation. In this confusion, you made a plan about how to stay safe in the world. Throughout your lifetimes, you used this plan over and over. Now a once-simple decision becomes a network of negative thoughts and feelings that culminates in the Grave of Buried Feelings. The plan, of course, doesn't work, but that doesn't stop you from making the attempts to be safe. These control plans sound like this:

I have to be perfect and make everything perfect (in order to stay safe)
I have to help others (in order to stay safe)
I have to accomplish and achieve (in order to stay safe)
I have to search and search for love (in order to stay safe)
I have to observe and think (in order to stay safe)
I have to make everything secure (in order to stay safe)
I have to make everything fun (in order to stay safe)
I have to control people (in order to stay safe)
I have to agree with everyone to keep the peace (in order to stay safe)

Control plans are funny things. When they are born in us, they are filled with promise of solution. Unfortunately, they don't produce lasting or satisfying results. They cannot do so because they are created from fear, isolation, and loneliness, and anything authored from fear can never bring lasting, satisfying results.

We discovered that the "little i", the ego, is our personality, our own collection of thoughts and feelings and that our Soul is the I AM, composed of the Divine aspects of Love, Wisdom, Beauty, Harmony and Understanding. Your Soul, now divided into its male and female qualities, produces the personality, a Divine Child. This is you, the personality. The personality is the one that has to contend directly with physical life, and it is the personality that loses its way. It is vital, then, to heal the faulty thoughts and feelings of the Spiritual male and female and Divine Child in order to create a life based on truth, rather than on fear and uncertainty.

The Origin Process takes two sessions. The first one is called the soul clearing, wherein you discover the faulty beliefs that Your Divine Male, Divine Female (Soul) and Divine Child (personality) chose because of the original separation from God. You follow the path of your Divine Male and Female from the Garden of Eden to their arrival upon earth. You hear their thoughts and reactions to each other in physical bodies. When they create a child, the Divine Child, you further investigate the beliefs each of them chose to take on. When those feelings have been opened and healed, the Spiritual Family (Divine Male, Female, and Child) is able to go directly to God and ask all the questions they have ever needed to ask. They receive answers that bring clarity, understanding, peace, and most of all, a healed, rejoined relationship with God. While each of them—Divine Male, Divine Female, and Divine Child— is the one asking the questions, those very questions are, of course, your deeply-held sorrow and fear about life and God. When they emerge, the questions are familiar because you have held them vaguely or openly all your life. What is new and powerful and healing are the answers. As a result, you deeply understand that original separation and a new peace spreads within you. Ann, a client in her sixties, had always felt she should never have been born. This belief didn't surface during Purification and we found only a little piece of it in the Caged One where she *knew* she was worthless. In the Origin, however, it all came out during her conversation with God. The Spiritual Female held all the pain. I'll never forget Ann's painful wail when she asked God a simple question. "Why?" It took a while for the sobbing to cease. When she shared God's answer, her whole energy opened like a flower. The answer, simply, was, "I never left you." It was all she needed to know.

The second session, the ego clearing, is where you discover your control plan to make people love you. After all, we miss terribly the feelings of love and oneness. To retrieve them and ensure our emotional safety we decide upon another control plan, which also doesn't work. That control plan is identical to the above list except in the paretheses, each one reads "in order to get love." Through an experience in this lifetime, you discover the method you chose to accomplish this. Looking over your life, you become aware of the constant failure of that plan to produce anything except more separation. Once you see the fallacy of your choice and understand how it only brought you more pain and separation, you become free to make better choices. Now, you are free to love and be loved, not out of fear but out of love.

How do you know if this is the process you need? In your life, you will be trying to come to grips with separation, isolation, and survival fears in some way. Far too often, we take those devastating feelings for granted. "Of course," you say, "everyone feels empty, lost, and concerned about 'making it.' Don't they?" Well, yes, but not because it is the way things are but because those feelings arise from a buried depth of negative knowledge that you are isolated in this world and very much at risk.

The results of the Origin process are the ability to feel safe in your life, to love and be loved without neediness or an agenda, and to have a real relationship with your Divine Creator. You will no longer pray in a begging fashion or fear that God will somehow rip the rug out from beneath your feet. You'll know that you can trust the Divine because you now understand that *all your faulty thoughts have been created by you.* Your sense of personal power is growing. This isn't a "bully" type of power or a muscle-flexing power or a desire to control others, but rather, it is a fantastic flow of such strength and understanding that you can stand upright inside of yourself and claim your life as your own creation. In that claim, you truly understand that you attract into your life *exactly what you are thinking.* You also understand that the flighty, fleeting, momentary thoughts you have are not the ones that attract negativity. The thoughts with that much power are the ones you buried. Those are the ones that poison your life. Now, with each step of your healing, you gain the understanding and insight to create your life anew with loving and positive thoughts and feelings.

If that isn't power, then what is?

# CHAPTER 8

## *Divine Mother*

Whereas the Origin process deals with the masculine face of God, called the Father, the Divine Mother process deals with the feminine face of God called the Mother. These two sides, or faces, of God have their counterparts on earth in the form of our parents. As children, we see our Mother as God. She can keep you in her womb or not; she can feed and hold you or not. She can love and cherish you or not. She nurtures and disciplines you, and she has great control and direction over your life. Her influence is deep because she is the giver or withholder of love. As children, we need her love. Without love, we cannot thrive. Without loving care, we cannot survive. She holds all the cards.

And we know it.

Naked and alone in the world as infants, we are far from helpless. We assess the situation quickly from the moment of our first breaths. What do I have to do to survive? This is our most basic of instincts. We reach out with our energy (our arms being a bit wobbly) and we create cords of energy and attach them to our mothers, much as climbers attach ropes to each other and the cliff they are climbing on in order to stay safe.

The cords we create to attach to our mothers have the same purpose: safety in a huge world. They are very, very real. Your therapist can sense these cords with his or her hands. You are very aware of them intuitively, if not physically. I have heard people say, "When I am around my mother, I get a headache." We suppose it is because of the stress of the relationship, but in fact, it is from a cord of attachment. These cords are living energy, and they transmit thoughts and feelings from you to your mother and back again, like numerous umbilical cords. They are tiny telegraph wires that keep sending the same messages over and over and over. What are those messages?

When we are small and alone and reach out to mother for help, we are ready to make a deal: *Keep me safe and love me, and I will do whatever you want me to do.* We make all kinds of agreements with our mother to buy what we need. If we had money, we'd lay cash on the table. Lacking that form of exchange, all we have to bargain with is our behavior. For all our lives, unless we find and release the agreements, we behave with our mothers in ways that are inherently unhealthy because early on we felt helpless and the only way through this dilemma was to make a deal to obtain what we needed. For the most part, of course, we don't receive what we are looking for, not because our mothers are so awful they won't provide it, but we *created the cords from fear and fear cannot produce good results.* Besides, our mothers, too, have created cords with their own mothers and have not fulfilled those relationships either. The beat goes on, generation after generation, each attaching to the other through fear and misunderstanding until we are ready to sever those cords and release the inhibiting thoughts and feelings.

The mother-child relationship is such a frustrating relationship because even though in your eyes and heart your needs aren't met, you continue to give up parts of yourself in spite of the fact you've never received what you want. It is a fabulous moment when a client sees clearly and without blame their creative role in their relationship with their mother. Doors of love and forgiveness and understanding fly open. It is wonderful to realize that your mother is just a person with the same wants, needs, and frailties as yourself! She's not an ogre, even if her behavior has been reprehensible. She's just another fragile human caught in a web of fear and isolation. Gradually, Ro-Hun helps us take responsibility for our lives, placing the power to change our lives right back in our own hands.

Here are some examples of corded agreements and possible resulting behavior:

*I'll do everything I can to make you proud of me. Just see me.* This agreement would lead to feeling that you have to keep doing, achieving, and accomplishing. Maybe you'd have to earn a string of college degrees or rise to the top in your profession, but all the while, you feel unacknowledged, invisible, and invaluable.

*I'll take care of myself. You don't have to do anything. Just love me.* This agreement leads to an overpowering sense of responsibility. Just give you the task and consider it done. You'll do it all. This weighs heavily on your energy and pulls life force and vitality out of you. If you just do one more thing, you believe that she'll really love you.

*I'll be really good. I won't cry or ask for your attention or time. Just love me.* This agreement can lead to being a "people-pleaser" or being invisible. In either case, it results in a suppressing of personality, wants, needs, desires, even opinions in order to be seen and accepted.

These thoughts and more form the life-sucking attachment cords. These pleas and deals for love draw the life force out of you, keeping you and your mother frozen in a dynamic that, without recognition and healing, is carried with you throughout eternity. What a thought! Stuck to your mother in those disastrous behaviors throughout eternity! But unexamined and unnoticed, those cords travel with us through time and space, lifetime after lifetime. As a result, we carry into each life, into each new and fresh little baby body, the baggage of the last one with all those faulty thoughts and negative feelings that we used to unconsciously create our last life. For many, this sounds like a horror story. To those who are really listening, they hear the sound of hope! If you don't want to repeat anything you've already lived through—neglect, lack of love, emptiness, isolation, loneliness, fear, sadness, rage, and loss—then, if you attend to business and yank open that cesspool, you can be freed forever.

We'll take one of those corded attachment thoughts and follow it through to see how it might create in life. For whatever reason, you made the agreement, "I'll do everything I can to make you proud of me. Just love me," with your mother, and in infancy, she coos over you and thrills at your accomplishments. You assume all is well. Then, a sibling is born and her attention shifts. You are trying harder to earn her approval and not much is coming your way. You don't realize the pressure she is under handling two children. The corded attachment agreement is beginning to tremble within you. You start to try harder. One day, you are coloring a picture for Mommy. She is carrying your little brother and fixing dinner at the same time. He's been crying a lot that day, so you want to show her how good you are (trying to please her) and earn her love, which has been lacking. You finish the picture, slide off the chair so pleased with your efforts, and go to her. Just as you tug on her to get her attention, something happens on the counter that you cannot see. Mommy jumps back and shrieks, which starts your brother shrieking. Not knowing that something glass just exploded all over the counter, you continue tugging on her, saying, "Look Mommy." She turns to you, "Get out of here! There's glass all over. Go! Into the other room!"

Obviously, to your immature self, ignorant of what just happened on the counter, you believe that she doesn't love you and that there's no pleasing her! She refused you and your picture.

She refused your love. Nothing you can do will please her and earn her love; off you go, heartbroken. Even though she explains in a few minutes and hugs you, the damage is done. The corded agreement has taken over, so you redouble your efforts to gain her love and can never feel it because you know it can't happen. No logic in the world argues those thoughts and feelings away. As an adult, you can say, "Well, of course. Glass was everywhere and she was trying to keep me safe." But the little child in you remains caught in the pain of the moment and needs healing.

That same corded agreement could result in an even worse experience. Depending on the depth of your belief that you cannot please your mother and receive love, you might draw to you a physically or emotionally (or both) abusive mother. Our corded agreements with our mother follow us throughout lifetimes, if not discovered and healed. They also affect our relationship to ourselves as mother. Because we know that the energy called mother cannot be pleased, our own abilities to nurture and sustain love for others will be negatively affected. This is true whether we are a man or a woman because mother energy exists in both.

These cords attach from us to our mothers through our individual chakras. Chakras are energy centers in our bodies. These centers are a bit like USB ports where the cords attach between mother and child. A more expanded explanation of the chakras is found in Chapter 10. The therapist is skilled in feeling and handling these cords and is able to guide the client to discover where the cords are in their own chakras and how they have attached to the mother. Once the cords are located and understood, they are severed and removed appropriately and carefully, and the faulty thoughts and feelings are transformed.

You might think that a spiritual person—one who has been following a spiritual path for years and uses many spiritual tools—would have discovered and dealt with these cords. But that's not the case. They are buried and protected so deeply that you actually must seek them out. For example, one of my clients was quite a spiritual woman, having studied and meditated for years. She had gone through both Purification and the Caged One several years prior. Yet, in her conversations, I noticed that she frequently referred to her parents, especially her mother, as the cause of so many of her life's difficulties. This is not un-usual because of our unconscious need to protect those cords, even though they never have provided us with what we needed. Ultimately, I suggested she might benefit from the Divine Mother process. I shared with her the things I'd been hearing through-out our conversations. To her credit, she agreed to perform the process. The results were amazing as years of attachment and blame fell away. Her mother had already passed away, and so the clearing was especially profound as she felt her mother in the spiritual world become free from the cords as well. If a client's mother is still living, the client will notice a different relation-ship develop as he or she is able to approach his or her mother as an individual rather than a helpless child bound to the mother through fear.

This need for safety and love extends beyond our physical mothers to our Divine Mother, the Great Mother and nurturer of all human life. We send attachment cords to her as well, pleading to be loved and kept safe and promising in return to—what? Be good. Be spiritual. Do good works. Make everyone else impor-tant. Sublimate our natural human needs. Self sacrifice. The list goes on and on. With all this agreeing, we further separate from the nurturing Love of God, which is shared with us through the Divine Mother, and we separate it from our natural human needs. Under all this promising and unnatural behavior is the deep, deep fear that we cannot survive without making deals.

Out of fear, we attempt to lasso the Divine Mother and are off and running on lifetimes of self-doubt, self-renunciation, fear, and uncertainty, including the fear of God and all things Divine.

When we are in fear of the Divine Mother, we often cannot fully release our own mothers. I had a male client who had a terribly difficult childhood with his mother. Although we worked hard to find and release the cords with her, I felt the lack of depth in the healing that took place. There were releases, but I knew something was missing. We found it when he saw the Divine Mother. She appeared to him like a huge, black, ominous witch. He, a grown man, trembled on the table as he faced this fearsome creature. As we worked, locating and severing the cords, all of his fear of being controlled, overwhelmed, misunderstood, and blamed for everything came pouring out. His sobs wrenched my heart as he finally released his fear that God (in the form of the Divine Mother) hated him. He had gone through the Origin Process a few months earlier, but he hadn't touched this depth of pain with God the Father. It was God the Mother that brought it out. He looked ten years younger when we finished! This was such a profound illustration that through doing all the Ro-Hun processes, the client's skill to see and feel and his Strength of Light deepened with each inward step.

As if corded agreements to your mother and Divine Mother aren't enough, there is another Mother we might bind ourselves to—Mother Earth. What if she decides to blow up? Or reverse her poles? Or scour her face with tornadoes, hurricanes, floods, and fires? We'd better protect her! So, we form cords there as well. It is good to be a good steward of the earth, but not to the point of being tied to it. Go green, for sure. Do your part, but not out of fear. Fear cannot breed anything but itself. Love heals, lifts, and makes all things possible. Fear degrades, separates, and kills. Agreements with Mother Earth need to be explored so that guilt and any unhealthy sense of responsibility for the earth do not invade our consciousness and our sanity. Healed, we are able to be far more creative in our personal lives when it comes to respect and caring for the earth. In that energy, we are charismatic and can affect change. In our fear, we preach, frighten, threaten, and alienate those who could help us. Healing this convoluted relationship with the Mother energy frees us to be nurturing, gentle, inspirational, wise, and perceptive.

Through these last two processes, the healing with the Male/Female aspects of God is deep. Now, we have to address the healing of our own male and female. Unity with God must express itself on earth through internal unity and unity with another.

CHAPTER 9

# The Androgynous Process

When we enter the earth, our Oneness becomes divided as we have seen. Because the earth is a place of duality—up and down, in and out, above and below—our physical bodies must obey the law of duality, resulting in male and female bodies. The Garden of Eden myth supports this idea, wherein Adam and Eve are pure (naked) and living by the grace of God. Yet, the Garden of Eden is only a stopping point. Had creation stopped here, there would be no humans on earth because the Garden of Eden isn't a physical location, but an Astral one; that is, the Divine Idea of male and female were thoughts, creative ideas, before they became physical. The nature of the Female is to receive, so the Female receives the Wisdom of God and the Light of God and carries them in her heart. This is Eve filled with a forward motion. She has to know. She has to complete her mission to become physical. Therefore, she takes steps to complete our birth into matter; the female always gives birth. In the story, Adam and Eve become aware of their nakedness and cover themselves, which represents coming into the physical body. On the earth plane, we can no longer exist as pure energies and pure ideas, but to finish the act of creation, we have to take on a physical body. So, we do.

In that division, the illusion of separation begins and so does the war of the sexes. Each one has a job to do, but in this separation, each forgets the value of the other, consumed with his or her own fears and qualms about surviving in this world. He doesn't understand her. She is so inner and emotional and going on and on about "the relationship." She doesn't understand him. He is so distracted by the world and trying to figure things out in attempts to make everything work, ignoring "the relationship." The stage is set for internal division. Our feelings, emotions, sensitivity, and our abilities to create relationships, receive inspiration, and permit our genius to emerge (all the traits of feminine energy) are stuck in an unfulfilling and harmful relationship with the male. Our active mind, our ability to think and reason and create ways and means to accomplish our desires in the world, our power to express our Self (all the traits of our male energy) are stuck in an unfulfilling and harmful relationship with the female. From here, all we can create are unfulfilling human relationships fraught with confusion and misunderstanding.

What dynamics drive our internal marriage? What internal dialogue constantly runs under the radar inside us?

The process of discovering the male/female dynamics is very simple, but the results are powerful. In the Androgynous Process, we explore sets of rooms in which we find the male and female. By paying attention to the actions, feelings, and thoughts in the room, we uncover the hidden dynamics and attitudes that exist between the two of them. Then we bring them into a harmonious, balanced relationship. While those words are simple, the process is anything but simple. Therapist and client work to establish rapport, respect, and love between two people who, upon initial discovery, are at war with each other, either openly or covertly. This private inner war makes our relationships ill and sickens our relationship with ourselves.

Suppose we discover that your female in one dynamic is frightened of the power of the male. She cowers, terrified of taking a step or moving away from the perceived threat; this means that within you, your feelings, your sensitivity, your great receptiveness and nurturing abilities are stifled, thwarted, and afraid of expressing themselves in your life. Through this dynamic, you might be holding the faulty thought, "I am completely at the mercy of everyone else." Perhaps that thought has drawn you to an abusive male, whether it's your father, brother, friend, lover, or boss. That would be a direct result, but perhaps the results are more difficult to see. This thought could make you check and double-check your own decisions, fearful of taking a wrong step and being punished for it. You might see yourself as powerless in your job, having to take what the boss dishes out without asserting yourself. It might lead you into situations of being a prisoner, perhaps actually in jail or held in bondage in some way, unable to escape a domineering parent or the power of any authority. It could make you extremely religious, afraid of God's anger. It could turn you into a man-hater, regardless of whether you are a man or a woman. At the very least, it would create great internal doubt, fear, and personal debate, perhaps even self-hatred. What the thought does to you is unique to you. Add to the mix that you have been living lifetimes with that thought, and you begin to realize the depth of your own unhealthy creation.

Suppose in one dynamic, we find your male frozen and immobile, staring off into space, completely unaware of anything around him. The world could be blowing up and he wouldn't know it. His eyes are empty. No one is home. He's not even thinking; this means that within you, your great and powerful mind and mental abilities are frozen, unmoving, unthinking, and blank. How would that possibly look in your life? You might be aloof, disconnected from people, places, and things. Perhaps you live the life of a hermit or, at the very least, away from people and social interaction. Because of such vacancy and emptiness, it is possible you are abusive to those around you, not out of anger or rage but because they have no meaning to you and you dismiss them. You could be a person who comes home from work and isolates yourself with the TV or computer. You could be man or woman. You might be one-track-minded, but not in a helpful, focused way, but with tunnel vision. There would be great coldness and lack of caring; you might even live in disarray without noticing. Now, suppose that both of those dynamics— the frightened woman and the frozen man—were inside you and in the same room. In a session with a client, that is exactly what we discovered. The client, who happened to be a woman, related all too well with this inner frozen state. She could not make a decision about her next step in life. She just could not. All possibilities were frightening, so she buried herself in her work, focusing on it with all her might and trying to ignore the rest of her life. Her female energy was frightened, and her male energy disconnected. Her life was going nowhere, fast.

When we finally brought this client's male and female into balance, and they recognized and respected each other, the joy on my client's face was undeniable. She felt the inner union; she felt the strength of self return to her body. She actually felt her body and the energy flowing through it for the first time in a long time. It wasn't that she had a physical ailment that made her body numb, but she simply had not been aware of her body for years. When we discussed how this healing would change her life, she replied, "In every way possible!" She recognized that her desire for a love relationship could never be fulfilled as long as she had this internal division. She knew she would have stayed in her lackluster (but safe) job forever. At the end of the session, she felt strong, confident, and whole. Gradually, she made changes in her life, which ultimately led to a satisfying job. She had been working in an office cubicle, safe, frozen, and going nowhere. Following her Androgynous process, she rediscovered a long-hidden passion for photography. Following this new interest, she joined a photography club and met a man who shared her interests. While he did not become the man of her dreams, she was now swimming in a new world and open to giving and receiving love.

When our inner male and inner female cannot love and respect each other, where are we, the in-dwelling Soul, to turn? How are we going to follow our life path if our internal halves are stuck in separation, fear, and pain? For those who are in relationships, this process reveals the underpinnings of the relationship, opens it to a new view, and the client is able to see his or her own attitudes played out through personal relationships. The door is now open for a true relationship to develop because the client is aware of his or her responsibility in the dissatisfactions of the relationship. Without addressing the male and female within, what might we expect? For one, we can spin forever from one relationship to another, enduring the same patterns repeatedly, wondering why there are no good relationship possibilities out there. We can make plans, sabotage them, and blame others for our failures. We can dream our dreams and let them blow away in the wind because, without an internal union, we don't have the strength, vision, or passion to carry them out.

As a client progresses from one Ro-Hun process to the next, the look and texture of the processes refines. Much drama and turmoil is discovered during the Purification and Caged One processes. Once the client gains spiritual strength, the level of drama and angst necessary for the client to see, understand, and release decreases considerably. This mark of progress indicates that the client is now more skilled in how to work with the energy of discovery. This is not to say that the healing and releases of the advanced processes are less impactful. They are, in fact more profound and amazing because the client is now able to plumb the depths of the Grave of Buried Feelings with more courage, dedication, and delight. Yes—delight! Once a client realizes that the deeper he or she dives into the Grave, the freer and fuller his or her life becomes, the client becomes eager to continue to the next process.

# CHAPTER 10

## *Seven Visions of Self*

In this very beautiful and inspiring process, Seven Visions of Self, you develop, heal, and mature the seven major archetypes within, resulting in seven strong, healthy self-images through which you can create harmony. But first, let's talk about these archetypes and why they need healing.

According to Carl Jung, the great pioneer of human consciousness and behavior, archetypes are universal psychic structures that underlie all human experience and behavior. Jung began the quest to understand archetypes, and through the intervening years, we have deepened our understanding of them. Many archetypes, or consciousness models, exist. Through them and with them we grow and evolve. Their names are familiar: the Warrior, the Victim, the Lover, and the Savior, for example. Mother is an archetype, as are Father and Child. We have certain ideas of each of these personality aspects, and we live our lives dependent upon our idea of each of them. If we are caught in the Warrior archetype, we wage war—whether that is war on another country, war on another person, war against certain ideas, war against someone of another color or religion, war for the sake of profit, or war to save the environment. All wars represent the Warrior archetype operating in consciousness. Not very evolved, is it? Yet it is within every one of us. Every person can and will wage some kind of war when they need to feel a sense of power; the Warrior archetype gives us a feeling of personal power. Who hasn't seen the PTA mom waging war? Who hasn't seen the environmentalist waging war? Who hasn't seen the preacher waging war? No matter how we describe it, the Warrior archetype behaves the same way in every individual. It fights to feel power.

Some wars are good, you might say. Bringing people to God or saving the spotted owl are good goals. Any time the warrior archetype is engaged, someone has to lose—that is the nature of the archetype, win and lose. That is certainly not spiritual. That is certainly not the consciousness that will heal itself and find peace, goodness, love, and wisdom. The Warrior will push and push and insist that someone else lose. No goodness comes from the Warrior, no matter how glorious the goal. When anyone has to lose, everyone has lost because raw power is dominating and a Warrior who has either won or lost will turn to look for another fight, resulting in endless agony for everyone.

The flipside of the Warrior is the Victim. We looked at the victim archetype in the Purification process. We looked for all the places where you perceived victimhood and took on personal beliefs that sealed your fate as a victim, beliefs that continued repeating because of the internal decision that you are, and were, a victim. Not very pretty are they? In one sense, you defeated part of the Warrior archetype. Everyone, no matter how they appear to you, carries the Victim archetype. It is inescapable. Sometimes the Victim archetype causes the Warrior to emerge violently. It probably doesn't seem possible that some of our greatest bad guys in history were reacting to their Victim archetype, but those who are power hungry likely feel powerless.

God is also an archetype—the model of the Loving Parent, the Creator, and the Bringer of Eternal Life. Throughout the ages, God has taken on different faces and roles, and if we really look, we find that God (our image of God) evolves as we evolve. In the Old Testament, for example, God was a God of wrath, judgment, and whim, demanding praise and worship. After the Christ Event, we began to perceive God as a parent of love, forgiveness, and compassion; our archetype called "God" evolved. But, did God evolve, or did we remove some of our own abusive, power-ridden, fearful ideas, and witness God in a different fashion? Some gods have demanded sacrifice, both animal and human. Others have demanded tithing one's wealth to god. Ever wonder why God needed money, or goats, or vegetables? Could it be our own un-evolved perceptions of the Divine at work?

You have already met two powerful archetypes: God as Creator in the Origin Process and Mother in the Divine Mother process. In the Seven Visions of Self, we concentrate on a set of archetypes associated with our energy centers, which are called chakras. "Chakra" is a Sanskrit word meaning "wheel". This ancient term refers to various circular-shaped energy centers located within the body along the spine. The chakras extend energetically about three feet out from the body. They connect our emotional, mental, and spiritual bodies with the physical one, creating wholeness or unity between body and soul. These centers metabolize, if you will, divine spiritual substance and draw that substance into the physical body, linking body and soul in a powerful union. Because we have these links between body and soul, it would seem that enlightenment is at hand. Yes and no. Yes, our spirit is ready and willing to flow completely into our lives, and no, it cannot until the mental and emotional bodies are healed.

The Seven Visions of Self process addresses each chakra and its archetype, revealing and healing the faulty thoughts and feelings that effectively block the Light of Spirit from being fully present in our lives. Think of our Negative Reactive Selves as masks we have placed over our chakras, filtering the goodness of our spiritual energy through the muck and mire of our faulty thoughts and feelings. What actually comes through? A distortion of our true Self, and each of us calls that distortion "me."

The Root chakra, located at the base of the spine, is the home of the archetype called the Presence. It is through our Presence that the rest of us flows into our life. When the Presence is filled with doubt and fear, how could something as wonderful as unconditional love or acceptance or vision flow into our lives? The Presence is *how I present myself to the world*. This is the only visible archetype -- the visible "I". If that Presence is clouded by pain and fear, little beautiful energy will be flowing into the life. The Presence lives in its own reality, so to speak, and is not even aware that other aspects of the Self (archetypes) exist. The Presence fails to realize that it ought to be working with them instead of being self-centered. However, an unenlightened Presence has no idea of the existence of anything or anyone outside of itself and, therefore, does not live in cooperation with the other archetypes. This kind of self-focus in the Presence prevents inner exploration, self-knowledge, and internal partnership because the Presence focuses on the world, not the rest of the Self. When healed and in relationship to the entire Self, this chakra brings Spirit into matter. It can accomplish this because it is associated with the physical body and all the other archetypes express through it.

The next chakra is the Spleen, or Sacral, chakra, and it is located about two inches below the navel in the belly region. The archetype associated here is the Emotional One because this chakra is the home of the emotional, or desire, body. Just as the Presence is self-focused, so is the Emotional One. It can be volatile or numb or any combination of emotional expression in between. It is highly charged even if the emotions are repressed. Unhealed, it is immature and sometimes carries great and frightening power. Who hasn't felt the raw, scary force of someone else's Emotional One? Who hasn't felt the raw, scary force of his or her own Emotional One, when snared in anger, rage, grief, sorrow, or fear? This archetype says *this is how I feel about myself in the world*. Healed, this archetype is the Vital Energy of God, capable of funding any creative idea with the juice needed to bring that project into manifestation. This archetype brings profound excitement and deep satisfaction.

Going up the body, the next chakra is in the solar plexus, and it is called the Achiever. It can be a taskmaster, never allowing a moment's peace. There is always something else to do and it can drive us forward, relentlessly. That is not to say there is any satisfaction; there is none because the purpose of the Taskmaster Achiever is to keep doing. On the other hand, the Achiever can be filled with doubt, powerlessness, or a sense of no control over life. In this state, it becomes the Underachiever and fills our ideas and projects with powerlessness. This solar plexus archetype is about *how I achieve in the world*. The Achiever is rather cold because it is located in the home of the mental body, and it is focused on accomplishing ideas rather than expressing feelings. As volatile as the Emotional One can be, that is how cold and reserved the Achiever can be when caught in its own self-focus. Healed, this archetype is capable of bringing any inspired idea into fruition through the ability to plan and to execute those plans with clarity and precision while maintaining a healthy balance between doing and resting.

Now we come to the Master chakra, the Heart. The Heart is the home of the One Who Cares, i.e., unconditional Love. This is the only archetype that is aware of all the others and the only one that strives, often without help or recognition, to bring harmony, balance, wisdom, and love to the whole being. The One Who Cares helps us to survive in the face of great odds and keeps us filled with hope for a better tomorrow; it encourages us not to give up when life is tough. The One Who Cares is the embodiment of God living within us. The Heart chakra is our Soul's earthly Home. When a client is ready to experience the Seven Visions of Self, they are first introduced to the One Who Cares so that they can partner with it in healing the other archetypes. When the client meets Unconditional Love face-to-face within, it is a magnificent moment. That, in itself, is a momentous healing, but it is just the beginning. The One Who Cares says *I AM Love*.

The next center is in the throat and is called the Throat chakra. The archetype here is the Expresser. This archetype's thought is, *this is how I express myself in the world*.Even though it is located in the throat, the expression of self isn't limited to verbal expression, but it includes all forms of personal expression, including the manner of dressing, the way personal space is or is not decorated, how ideas are shared or not, and facial expressions and body language, among others. When our ego—comprised of the root, spleen, and solar plexus chakras (Presence, Emotional One, and Achiever)—is filled with faulty thoughts and feelings, the Expresser is severely limited in its realm of influence and cannot function with any clarity and impact. It can express clearly neither the ego self nor the spiritual self; it exists in a state of limbo, a no-man's-land. If the Expresser is fully expressing the faulty thoughts and negative feelings of the ego, it can become filled with criticism, manipulative persuasion, and lies. The Expresser cannot fully function while the Presence, Emotional One, and Achiever remain caught in negative ideas, painful feelings, and self-focus. This archetype is extremely powerful, for when it is healed of its masks and joins cooperatively with the others, it expresses our Divine Attributes of Love,Wisdom, Harmony, Beauty, and Understanding. While this may sound too heady for real life, the fact is, such an individual becomes appropriately charismatic, approachable, and very down-to-earth.

In the center of the forehead is the Third Eye chakra, home

to the Visionary. This is a fabulous energy to have—the magic of Vision. The function of the Visionary is, *this is how I see my purpose*. If the Visionary is clear and connected to all the other chakras, there is insight and clarity of goals and an expanded purpose—one that includes not only the Self but all of mankind. Mostly, however, this archetype is not clear and connected, but it is disconnected and living in its own kind of reality, removed from what is happening in life. Therefore, it is unable to be the guide it is meant to be. With a disconnected Visionary, we might dream great dreams, but we have little or no ability to make those dreams a reality. Healed, this archetype perceives, knows, and understands that all is perfect as it is and that the Divine Plan affords all the space, time, and opportunities necessary for each soul to awaken to its full Divine Potential.

At the top of our head is the Crown chakra, and the archetype is the Divine Persona. One would assume that the Divine Persona would have no problems, but that is not so. A Divine Persona archetype, while carrying our deep and permanent connection with God, can also be a way to escape our physical lives, preferring instead to spend time in the pursuit of higher knowledge or in piousness. A Divine Persona archetype could make us ungrounded, unreal, and difficult to understand or reach. We might feel lost and adrift in a world that seems cold, aloof, and confusing. Without this depth of Oneness, we navigate life haphazardly, often relying on external help from anything from drugs to religious structures, that promise to provide this missing sense of connection. The knowing this archetype carries is *I AM*.

It is clear that these seven major archetypes need healing and balancing. They must meet each other, respect each other, and be willing to work with one another. For example, the Presence, without partnership with the others, is shallow and unable to express itself in terms other than "how do I look?" The Achiever frequently has very little respect for the Emotional One, and the Emotional One fears the Achiever's drive. Without respect for the Emotional One's vital power, the Achiever will work and work and work with little or no satisfaction or sense of accomplishment. Frightened of the Achiever's drive, the Emotional One won't lend its great emotional thrust to any project or involvement, causing ideas to fall flat without resolution. The union created through the healing and cooperation of the Presence, the Emotional One, and the Achiever is powerful and productive, providing a solid healthy Ego through which our Spiritual Self— the One Who Cares, the Expresser, the Visionary, and the Divine Persona—can flow. In addition, the union of the Expresser and the Visionary—in partnership with the One Who Cares and guided by the Inspiration and Creative Energy of the Divine Persona—leads to knowing that a human being can accomplish, feel, create, or enjoy anything. Because there is nothing we cannot accomplish and we have that firm base of a healthy ego, our Spiritual Purpose unfolds and we move toward it with confidence, resulting in deep and lasting contributions and creations in the personal world and the world at large. Completion of Seven Visions of Self results in deep personal confidence in ourselves as spiritually aware, present-on-earth human beings.

The Origin, Divine Mother, Androgynous, and Seven Visions processes have been strengthening your ability to look at yourself without blame, shame, guilt, or angst, allowing you to discover your own hand in your own painful creations through understanding your very own faulty thoughts and feelings. Now, and only now, you are ready to take the last step of pulling off all the illusions and faulty beliefs and discovering the four basic fears upon which you have built your life. This is a big statement, but one that is achievable. You are now ready for Constructs, Vaults, and Tanks.

# PART THREE: THE ROOTS

∽⚬∾

*Constructs*
*Vaults*
*Tanks*

∽⚬∾

*"When I let go of what I am, I become what I might be."*
—*Lao Tzu*

# CHAPTER 11

# Constructs, Vaults, and Tanks

Everything has a beginning, and your faulty thoughts and feelings are no exception. Although you have examined them in light of your experiences in this life, you didn't just begin in this life. You have been around for many lifetimes, and through all those centuries, have been expressing the only self you were aware of. Because you took on amnesia after your initial birth in this world, you have been wandering asleep and, therefore, creating life from that unaware place. When we are unaware of our Spiritual Nature and Love, we create from that which we are aware of, which is the polar opposite—physical nature and fear.

Through Constructs, Vaults, and Tanks, you discover the four basic thoughts (constructs), fears (vaults), and negative knowings (tanks) upon which you have built all your life. Yet, because of the work you have done through each of the processes up to this point, you have gained the ability to accept what you discover within yourself and to heal what you find. No longer are you afraid to see what lies within you. No longer are you crushed by realizations, emotions, or discoveries. Now you stand strong, knowing you are a spiritual being awakening to the Truth of yourself. You know without a doubt that you are able to create a fuller, richer, more satisfying life for yourself based on positive, fruitful ideas and feelings. You have come a very long way! Who is that person you used to be? Now it is time to get to the roots and remove them.

Constructs, Vaults, and Tanks are the roots. Everything you encountered in the other processes had their beginnings right here in the Constructs, Vaults, and Tanks. To this point, you have discovered:

- the Negative Reactive Selves of Purification
- the personal abuse and abuse of others in the Caged One
- your needy agreements with your various Mothers through the Divine Mother
- the depth of your belief in separation and your manipulative control plan discovered through the Origin
- the schism between your male and female discovered in the Androgynous
- the absolute lack of cooperation of your chakra archetypes in the Seven Visions of Self

All arise from the devastating illusions created in your Constructs, Vaults, and Tanks.

Constructs are thoughts, ideas, and beliefs that you know to be true. They aren't true, in actuality, but you believe them to be true because they are of your own creation. Vaults are fears that have been locked up and hidden away, and they are the power behind the Construct or idea. The idea (Construct) fueled by the fear (Vault) forces you to act in unbelievably predictable ways, and yet they are so unknown to you in their naked power that you have absolutely no idea they exist—even now after all the Ro-Hun therapy that you have experienced. Tanks contain deadly, toxic knowings, which are the result of the Construct married to the Vault— the idea married to the fear. These deadly knowings grind away within, leading you down paths of self-destruction, self-sabotage, and physical illness without you being aware of them.

To say "Tanks cause physical illness" is a shocking statement. To understand how that can be so, we need to understand the creative relationship of thoughts and feelings and their effect on our bodies. Thoughts, in and of themselves, are inherently impotent; they have no power. The power comes when a thought is married to an emotion. Emotions move, erupt, and drive us to accomplish whatever the thought is that we are holding. If we hold a hurtful thought and feel anger, we will move toward making that thought a reality. Because we are the ones holding the pain, we suffer the consequences. If we hold a positive thought and feel excitement, we benefit. In Constructs, Vaults, and Tanks, these thoughts and feelings are directed primarily towards ourselves with other people suffering as collateral damage. The power of the deadly knowing of the Tanks begins to wear down the body because the body has no protection against our personal onslaught. This is the terrible power of our negative emotions—self attacking self. Thus, unresolved emotions and their hurtful thought partners combine to create disease, illness, and debilitating conditions.

Together, these three consciousness spaces form the basis of your destructive thoughts and emotions. Every construct is linked to a specific vault and a particular tank, forming a column of misunderstanding, illusion, pain and suffering. For example:

### CONSTRUCT
*I have no*
*value*

### VAULT
*Fear of*
*Nothingness*

*TANK*
*Failure*
*Resulting in endless effort*
*to prove ones worth*
*in any way*
*possible*

This particular string of a Construct married to a Vault and resulting in a Tank (CVT) was part of one client's discoveries. She had always done things from a desire for people to see her, know her, and recognize her because she felt invisible. (I have no value and fear that I am nothing.) This resulted in extreme rebelliousness as an early teen, including a pregnancy and subsequent abortion that proved to be life-threatening. There were other harmful experiences including drunk driving and DUI arrests, partying, outrageous behavior, and taking risks. She did everything she could to combat her deep belief in her lack of value; she fought to keep the fear of being nothing at bay.

Tracing this particular CVT backward, so to speak, from the roots through the branches of the other processes, we can see the chain of beliefs at work through all the levels. On the Purification level, there was a great amount of blaming others—her parents, siblings, and teachers. When she was an adult, the blame shifted to her employers, her spouse, and the ubiquitous "they." "They" became responsible for much of her misery. In the Caged One, her self-abuse through the partying, drinking, and risks became evident, as did her abuse of others through chiding and deriding them about their shortcomings. In the Origin, her control plan was to control others with anger and force them to love her, which was translated in her mind, "If they see me, they love me". Her fear and anger towards God emerged, "Why did you DO this to me?"

In her Androgynous process, her female and male alternately took up power. In one discovery, the female was like the Sirens of mythology, luring the helpless male into unhealthy activities. In another, the male was like a warrior, beating the female into submission so that he could conquer others. Her relationship with her mother was heavily corded with the cord of "see me, see me, see me" bound together with another cord of "love me, love me, love me" through nearly every chakra. It was, to say the least, a tangled mess!

By the time she performed the Seven Visions of Self, she had done so much healing that her archetypes responded easily to the love of the One Who Cares. This was quite a relief for both of us because the road had been long and arduous. Yet, she still had to find the core, and she did so in Constructs, Vaults, and Tanks. Those discoveries helped her realize that she wasn't crazy or uncontrollable, which people had told her through the years. Her actions had reasons, rather than being the result of willful and random behaviors. There is peace in knowing we are not the patchwork quilt of behavior and emotions that we sometimes feel we are. There is sanity and order within us.

Four of these column-like CVTs create the last level of self-deception, self-torture, and self-delusion. While our Constructs are as individual as we are, all of us have the same four Vaults or fears (Fear of Nothingness, Fear of Failure, Fear of Death, and Fear of Abandonment) and the same four Tanks (Death Wish, Nothingness, Hatred, and Failure). As destructive as these are, the stunning part is that they are all illusions, internal games of make-believe we play with ourselves. When we first felt the pain and fear of earth life, like children, we raced into our imaginations and created alternative scenarios, albeit painful ones, to live through because the pain of the external life was even more acute. Using these internal make-believe scenarios, we were able to control the amount, depth, and scope of the pain we experienced, placing a barrier between us and the uncontrollable life around us.

The life event that caused my client to develop the string of the Construct of I have no value, the Vault of Fear of Nothingness, and the Tank of Failure was a past life. We found her as a baby in a dark, cold cave. She could see nothing and all she heard were the sounds of angry voices outside the cave. She had no idea why she was there. It was as if she went to sleep in one place, safe and warm, and awoke in the cold, hard cave. She was crying continuously, but no one came to her aid. From there, her Construct and Vault and Tank were born and part of her life path was set in motion.

Because these internal illusory beliefs are so strong and well formed, in the sessions we explore them as if each is a room. Rooms have definition and dimension, and within them, we find objects and the client in the form of a child. After all, when we are undeveloped psychologically and spiritually, we have no power, just like a child. And like a child, we use imagination to form our world. To a child, the world is not understandable. It is chaotic, painful, and frightening. In our consciousness infancy, we create alternative realities in order to survive and feel some form of control. These CVT rooms are not real and never have been real. The trouble is that we believe them to be real because we created them as protection against a world we couldn't control or understand.

External experiences cause us to go into our illusory spaces. For example, with my client, one trigger to put her into this string of CVTs was if someone didn't look her in the eye, which is a common experience. People don't always look us in the eye. So, she was in that CVT almost all the time. Hence, the behaviors described. Hence, a life that was difficult, sometimes even dangerous, and always confusing. Why don't they see me?

What we come to understand is that if we are not in touch with the Truth of ourselves, our Spirit, we are doomed to live in our four columns of CVTs over and over again—through our entire life. The truth is, if we are not living in Love, we are living in fear, and the CVTs are created through fear not love. This is sobering, especially when we realize that, to us, our CVTs are normal. To us, they are exactly how life really is. For example, with my client, the given, the truth of life, is that no one sees you, no one notices you, and you are invisible. To her, that would have been an obvious and factual statement.

In the CVTs, we understand the depth of our ability to create because we see the amazing destruction of these beliefs. For the first time in all the Ro-Hun processes, we anchor deeply our ability to create with Light and Love rather than with fear. Seeing, identifying, and understanding create the pathways to freedom. Yet, without having confronted your negative reactive selves repeatedly, without having connected to your Light, without having moved through the many levels of healing, you would not fully understand the depth and impact of the CVT level. Each level of Ro-Hun progressively strengthens, clears self-understanding, promotes forgiveness and love, and provides the power to reshape life in positive, fulfilling, and healthy ways.

CHAPTER 12

# *The End, Which Is the Beginning*

It is amazing to witness the depth of understanding and healing that a client attains when all the levels of Ro-Hun have been experienced. There is a maturity, peace, and self-acceptance that is beautiful to witness and feel. Eyes are clearer, hearts more open and flowing, and the ability to see their hand in creating their own life is profound, to say the least. Ro-Hun is a way of life. From this point on, the client knows all he or she needs to know about addressing his or her life experiences as they go forward. Clients know how to heal, why the healing is necessary, and they are unafraid to face themselves. Even more importantly, they are able to lovingly, and with wisdom, embrace themselves.

Will there never be problems in life? No. Of course, problems will arise. Is anger obliterated? Of course not. As humans, we are free to experience all our feelings without burying any of them. However, now the flush of anger can arise and almost immediately be understood, and a different response can be chosen. We are no longer a victim of ourselves, run around by an erratic and willful mind or wild, untamable feelings, we are what we are meant to be—the Master of our life.

Ro-Hun creates the open doors you have always wanted because it helps you close the doors that have always entrapped you. It is an end and a beginning.

Where can you find a Ro-Hun therapist? They are in many of the 50 states as well as countries around the world. To find the therapist near you, please visit Delphi University's website www.delphiu.com. There, you will find current listings of those therapists who are part of the Ro-Hun Professional Association. Click the tab "Healing and Renewal," and then click "Ro-Hun Professional." If no therapist is near you, consider going to Delphi University in McCaysville, Georgia, for your healing. The highly competent staff is ready to help you.

While on the website, I encourage you to explore it. Delphi has served for over 30 years to show the way for those who choose to follow a spiritual path. The school is dedicated to helping you discover and develop yourself using your spiritual gifts and abilities. To write me directly, please do so at janice33@janicehayes.com.

For your curiosity about Ro-Hun Therapy, for your decision to read this book, for the You that you are and always shall be, I am grateful. Whether you are aware of it or not, you are an amazing human being of Light and your Presence on this earth is necessary and important.

Peace be with you.

CHAPTER 13

# *What They Say About Ro-Hun*

While writing this book it became clear that others who have experienced the transformative power of Ro-Hun ought to have a voice. So, I reached out to some therapists and clients and asked if they might be willing to contribute their feelings and thoughts to this effort. I have chosen as wide a sampling as possible—men, women, geographic diversity, different ages— and yet you will hear a common song among them. These responses come from both practitioners and recipients of Ro-Hun Therapy. In many cases, the two are one and the same.

## David B. Robertson, Asheville, NC

Because I have observed the transformation of my life and the lives of my clients over the past few years, I know that Ro-Hun is one of the most significant portals of Grace to open for humanity in the past 2,000 years. Many of my clients' sense of wholeness had been fragmented by the experiences of sexual abuse. As they progressed through the structure of Ro-Hun, they witnessed the power of their love to forgive and heal the past, allowing them to reclaim their wholeness and live in the present. When they again felt their wholeness, miracles occurred. I've seen deformed legs begin to straighten, long-blocked menstrual cycles restored, relationships lovingly repaired, and questions of sexual identity finally resolved. Ro-Hun is a gift to humanity that is accelerating the evolution of group consciousness, and I am humbly grateful to be part of such a blessing.

**Audrey Delahunt, RhD, Oswego, NY**

Ro-Hun has been one of the single most significant healing modalities I have discovered, personally experienced, and facilitated. After studying alternative healing for 16 years, I have finally found something that moves my clients out of the energy that keeps them from knowing their divinity. In a matter of a few short sessions, I am seeing results that the clients themselves say they have not touched or healed, even after many years of traditional therapy and/or alternative healing methods.

Using energy and spiritual psychotherapy together has unearthed the avenue directly to the root cause of suffering. Once accessed, the client heals the wounds created and becomes free of the haunting subconscious that has kept them from knowing peace within. It feels like reuniting with God Itself, standing in your wholeness, and is nothing short of a miracle.

**Kathryn Tucker, RhD, San Jose, CA**

Over the last four to five years, my life has changed dramatically. Some changes have been sudden and others more gradual, but all of it has been amazing.

My own journey with Ro-Hun has helped me find answers that I was unable to find in traditional therapy. That's not to say that traditional therapy doesn't have its place; it can be an extremely helpful resource for many of us, and it has helped me a great deal at different times in my life. I was left, however, with the realization that it wasn't enabling me to change my life, so much as find a way to live with what I had going on. I had questions without answers and it felt like I had been told that was how it was going to be. Ro-Hun empowered me to understand, work through, and change my life in a relatively short period of time. It helped me to see much deeper into my subconscious, to the root of the issues.

I have balance. Balance in my energy system, balance between my engineering career and my calling as a therapist. Now, I know when I need to balance things with art, yoga, or just some time on my own. I still enjoy the hi-tech world, but I love the other side of my life, and most of all, I love that they are no longer separate from each other and conflicting. I no longer feel like a hostage in my own life.

As a therapist, I experience the amazing honor of being a catalyst that helps a client to take control of his or her life. I love watching clients make the connections between decisions they made in the past and how their lives are playing out today. As the understanding grows, so does the freedom. I have watched imagery move from pre-defined ideas that have been handed to them by society in various forms to the freedom of expression that comes from knowing that we are the creators of our own universes, and it can look exactly how we would wish it to be.

### Paul Miller, PhD, RhD, San Jose, CA

In San Jose, California, the heart of Silicon Valley, the left analytical brain rules. Trying to encourage a client to relax his or her logical mind and allow the right abstract mind to float free of constraints is not easy. The temptation to question what appears in their imaginations and its relevance to their lives can mean that the intuitive senses become stifled and the inner guidance becomes lost. With a degree in Physics and Electronics and a PhD in Engineering, I can relate to this very well. I have empathy for people who have a dominant left logical brain.

However, with courage and fortitude, the results [of Ro-Hun Therapy] start to show themselves. I remember the turning point for me came when I stopped editing what I saw and began telling the therapist my inner pictures, all the while thinking, "Well I am going to tell you exactly what I see and sense and let's see what you do with that." That of course is when things started to change for me because whatever I threw at the therapist, they worked with it and things started to change. It always makes me smile when I see my clients following the same path. After the results have come through, the next step involves explaining and elaborating with the client what surfaced in the session. For me, this is the magic moment when the client joins the dots and I see the realization and understanding appearing on his or her face.

As a therapist, I have seen results vary from good to quite amazing, including physical healings, an addiction stopping there and then, and finding an inner peace in interacting with friends and family. One client had been in traditional therapy for several years but had never connected to the emotions concerning the suicide of the client's father. Two hours into the Ro-Hun process, the client was well and truly connecting to the suppressed emotion. During the same session, the client had an intuitive piece of knowledge come to them concerning the suicide, something they did not know. Later, upon questioning family members, they discovered the information was, indeed, true.

I believe that if one has the courage and fortitude to step outside one's box and face down whatever is ready to surface, then Ro-Hun gives them the tools to know that they do not need to stand there alone, wondering what to do now that closet is open and the skeleton is rattling away.

## Lisa Fraine, PhD, RhD, RN, CNM, AHN-BC, MS Midwifery, Saratoga Springs, NY

The effects of Ro-Hun Therapy have altered my life in ways that I am still learning to understand. In 2003, my life was in ruins; my marriage, my life, and my spirit were broken. I turned to Ro-Hun Therapy, and now, nine years later, my life is moving in a direction of joy. My family is whole. My husband and I reconciled with the intention of forming a more loving union.

Through Ro-Hun therapy, I learned that my *perception* of my circumstances was distorted and that I could never be "broken." I learned to accept whatever the circumstances were, to take responsibility for my contribution to them, and to create from a different space. It was really quite simple when I realized that my life was the result of *my* thoughts and my feelings.

I continue to grow every day, using Ro-Hun techniques to continue allowing my spiritual nature to emerge. Ro-Hun is a practical part of my daily life. Now, as life's lessons present themselves, I have a wonderful tool with which to address them.

I was so moved by the results of the Ro-Hun process that I became a facilitator of Ro-Hun Spiritual Psychotherapy, completing through the Doctoral level at Delphi University in 2009. As I learned, I created a new life for myself because I am no longer willing to repeat destructive, useless patters. My purpose is to hold the Light to help others find their inner strength to go within and look at their internal chaos, confusion, and pain. I love helping them make sense of a lesson, integrating new and joyful energies into their lives because of self-understanding.

It is an honor to stand with another through the Ro-Hun process and watch the ego grow, allowing itself to merge with the Soul, creating the wholeness of the human experience that is possible in this dimension. Together with God, I walk a sacred journey, and I have been blessed to have Ro-Hun as a co-creative part of my life. I have a Life, a joyful Life, because of this process.

## Clar Cline, Surprise, AZ

I was fortunate to experience Ro-Hun twice. Both sessions were lengthy and thorough. Many of my "blocks" were removed, and I feel they are still gone; it has been about nine months. One of the issues solved for me was why I never cry anymore. We discovered it originated in my childhood (when I cried all the time) and traced it to a very tragic experience I had at the age of 20. I am now 57. I discovered that my ability to cry is one of the sensitivities I arrived with in order to fulfill my purpose. Since my Ro-Hun sessions, I have cried on appropriate occasions, and sometimes, even when I am not sure why. I just let the tears come and realize that it is okay to cry. It is part of who I am. It is safe. It is necessary. It is a form of cleansing for me.

There were many other issues addressed in the sessions. Relaying all of them would take pages! Ro-Hun has left me feeling more vulnerable, but in an extraordinary way, I am also stronger. I feel more freedom. I no longer worry or wonder what others are thinking about me. I seem to know that what others say does not need to be taken personally. I stand in my own space, feeling safe and secure. The last session I had was spiritually uplifting. I can only describe it as total peace. A feeling of complete acceptance and feeling connected with everything. Ro-Hun is an energy work that has filled me with contentment and joy.

## Alyson Tuxworth, Reiki Master, Bermuda

I first experienced Ro-Hun when I was visiting Delphi University in Georgia, for a metaphysics class. I didn't know much about Ro-Hun other than that it was a transformational therapy that would help me to be rid of the negative baggage of faulty thoughts and patterns I had been carrying throughout my life. Boy did I have a lot of those! The first process I went through was a Cleanse. I felt a little nervous going into the session, but I was quickly put at ease by my therapist. I lay down on a massage table with a light blanket over me. The room was candlelit and the feeling was that of being safely cocooned. The session was gentle, and we moved at a pace that I set, but at the same time, my therapist did push me ever so lovingly to really get in touch with what I was feeling. We worked through feelings of fearfulness, helplessness, unworthiness, and judgment. Some things were really hard to look at, and there were a few tears as I released them. It was strange because although I didn't want to continue to live with these negatives selves, and I wanted to release them, it was hard for me to do because I had been living with them for so long. They had been all that I thought I knew. But release we did, and I cannot begin to express how light I started to feel. This session also opened a huge doorway in my relationship with my parents. For the first time in my life, I really understood them and could forgive them for things that I had experienced as a child.

The other thing that was really quite amazing was that I actually came into contact with my inner child. I had always thought "oh, inner child stuff—yeah, right—whatever." Ro-Hun had me connecting and engaging with my inner child. I found the little me living in so much fear it was heartbreaking. When we helped her feel love and assisted her with releasing the baggage that she had been carrying for so long and never understood, it was liberating and freeing! When I returned to Bermuda, I decided to go through the Purification process. This was life changing for me. The deep, emotional cleansing through each chakra helped me release more negative selves and connect with my higher self. I literally looked different at the end of this process!

I followed up with a Skim session when I returned to Delphi

for more discovery and releasing. This was becoming deep—literally! It was great. A few months later, I went through The Caged process back in Bermuda. This process was all about patterns of self-abuse and self-sabotage and, how I used the same energy to abuse those in my life —was that life changing or what?! Oh my gosh, I never even realized what I was doing to others. That wasn't easy. At the end of this process, all I can say is that I felt empowered and free! It was the most difficult process to go through, and it did leave me feeling quite exhausted, but in a good way. This work went very deep and was worth every moment. At the end of this session, my therapist assisted me with building a beautiful bridge to my new life, a life that I chose filled with everyone and everything that I had ever wanted—all the joy and peace I craved. It was truly lovely.

Ro-Hun has helped me clear those blocks that have stood in the way of me living a life of joy, love, worthiness, and self-empowerment. This is a life changing process; it's real and gritty and can be very ugly, but at the same time, it is also loving, gentle, and soft. I always say that it's like having years of psychotherapy on the Indy 500 Speedway—it's fast and works right away. I can't recommend Ro-Hun enough. It is nothing short of life changing.

### Dr. Jennie Mills, RN, MS, PhD, Phoenix, AZ

My Ro-Hun experience as a client: I remember awakening in a recovery room after my third cancer surgery before the age of 40, knowing that I was self-destructing my life. It took decades of pursuing healing for myself before I arrived at the Ro-Hun Purification table. Seeking Ro-Hun actually felt like a "last chance" effort to heal what felt like an empty broken hole within me. If there would be a visual of how I felt, it would be that of a patchwork quilt covering over an empty space. Each patch represented some healing endeavor that healed some small part of sadness, grief, shock, anger, or fear along my relentless path. I believed I was broken. I'd even had therapists and practitioners tell me that "I needed a lot of work." I believed that some things just couldn't be healed. I was certain that there might be a spiritual connection for others and equally certain there was no God for me. After all, I'd seen evidence in so many books, seminars, classes, and healing rooms and tables that others had spiritual experiences and spiritual connection. Authentic spiritual connection and emotional healing hadn't happened for me.

It took less than 20 minutes into my first Ro-Hun Purification session to dispel the above beliefs about my healing and myself! I'd simply forgotten who I was, a spiritual being living an earthly existence. I continued my healing through every Ro-Hun process and emerged 18 months later feeling whole, complete, and "done." Gone was the unrelenting seeking.

My Ro-Hun healing efforts manifested in my life dramatically, and they continue now, years after I began my Ro-Hun healing journey. My friends and family remarked at the loss of that hard, angry, scowling, sharp edge I had carried. I found myself not judging others, having empathy for where they were in their lives instead of rejecting or avoiding them, or even worse, belittling them. I stopped sniping and using words to wound my husband when he had done absolutely nothing wrong. And, most importantly, I peacefully walk in my life partnered with Oneness and God, effortlessly, at ease in love and sureness. That empty hole is now Wholeness and the patchwork quilt is gone. I am at peace, active and vibrant, myself. What more could anyone want? I found that which I had been seeking: Wholeness with ease.

My Ro-Hun experience as a therapist: I have spent three decades of my life becoming traditionally educated with advanced

Master's and Doctoral degrees as a Registered Nurse, Psychiatric Nurse Practitioner, and Clinical Psychologist. I spent another decade becoming certified in at least 20 non-traditional complimentary energy healing modalities, including Advanced Hypnotherapy, Breath Therapy, Energy Medicine, and Energy Psychology.

A year after completion of the Ro-Hun Doctoral program and the Metaphysical Doctoral program from Delphi University, I had the opportunity to evaluate my therapy healing practice in depth. Skilled in so many helpful techniques and processes, I was startled to find that I had done nothing but Ro-Hun or the advanced processes from Delphi for months and months! I was advising and selecting Ro-Hun therapy over all other processes for the emotional and spiritual healing of my clients. Why? Because I knew that Ro-Hun therapy works better than any other process on the planet. Results are enduring, accessible, and rapid for clients. I wanted that for myself. I'm joyous at being able to deliver that to my clients.

### Eric Meyers, MA, Asheville, NC

Ro-Hun gets to the heart and root of unconscious issues. For the nine-hour purification this week, I was taken on a guided tour, an amazing journey into my psyche, illuminating everything with a sword of light. Powerful forgiveness and understanding, peace, and loving acceptance of everything—give yourself freedom, you deserve it.

### Bonnie Decker, Roswell, GA

It has been said that before one's reality can change, there must be a change in consciousness. Ro-Hun Therapy shifted my consciousness and my reality changed. It is the therapy for awakening! It takes courage and conviction to do Ro-Hun Therapy because it is not a therapy one tries, it is a therapy one lives.

In sharing my testimony here, it took some effort to re-member the woman who first arrived at Delphi University for healing. I used to identify myself as a survivor. I was born in an energetic of fear, cloaked in defensiveness, ensnared in vic-tim consciousness, and clinically diagnosed with post-traumatic stress disorder from childhood, among other things. I was a bit obsessive compulsive, somewhat of a control freak, and could not be in the vibration of love without crying. The underlying questions within me when I entered a room or any new experi-ences were, "Is it safe? Am I safe?"

I had already done both traditional and non-traditional ther-apies years prior, read countless books on recovery, listened to a multitude of speakers on the topics of enlightenment and heal-ing, but ultimately, I relied on my faith in God wholeheartedly as my source of survival and guidance. All my past therapeutic work laid the foundation for the deeper work of Ro-Hun.

After the first session, I knew Ro-Hun therapy was the right choice because I experienced some immediate relief and felt peace. I must admit that when I first began the Ro-Hun work, I did not know what to expect; however, I persisted and complet-ed the Ro-Hun processes over a four-year period. Each process cleared and anchored qualities that enhanced the next process. With each process, I grew stronger. Vulnerability was transmut-ed to love, empowerment, integration, harmony, understanding, clarity, wisdom, and even joy. These higher qualities were all there; everything in the way simply needed to be removed. This was the deepest work I had ever done, and the most significant. I am so very grateful to my therapist for being the light that guided me on this transformational journey. I so appreciate her love, clarity, wisdom, and tenacity when necessary.

Ro-Hun touched the very core of me—both my heart and my soul. When I first began, I thought expressing emotion was a sign of strength until I discovered that the true power and strength was the Light of me. I learned to receive love, which had been perceived as pain and betrayal in the past. I learned to recognize when I "fell from grace," and I was able to identify the disqualified thoughts and feelings reflecting in my reality. There were moments of real tenderness that were a new experience for me. Yet, upon reflection now, I see the love was always there. There was just a mountain of darkness in the way and, yet, sometimes what I thought was a mountain of darkness turned out to be a puff of smoke. There were challenging times, times I felt that I was fighting for my very life. At those times, I resisted fiercely in an attempt to cling to what I knew as real because it was my only identification. After all, when born into victim consciousness reality, what other reality was there? How was I to be in the world now?

In the end, I broke through the constructs of the mind, the vaulted misperceptions of my heart, and the tanks of feeling within where I was imprisoned. This last process opened new doors and brought choice, opportunity, and freedom into my life. Through Ro-Hun, all that inhibits full realization and creative expression is neutralized. I am alive!

These days the mirror of my reality is one of love, support, freedom, joy, and peace. My greatest awareness is that I am happy, every day. I find myself humming around the house and experiencing joy in the simplicity and beauty of life, like hearing a hummingbird's chirp for the very first time. Life flows. There is nothing I can't face, and I find each experience a reflection of my newly anchored understanding and truth through the Ro-Hun processes. With this deeper understanding, my level of compassion has deepened. My heart overflows with love and gratitude. I am awake and aware. In work, I am a clearer channel and am more available to my clients' needs. I feel unencumbered. When life's challenges appear, and they do, I can choose my response. Sometimes I falter and even fall. Still, I know what to do. I possess the Ro-Hun tools to pick myself up and facilitate that change in consciousness, and that is empowering on its own. It is my hope—through sharing some of my story and these insights—that you will consider Ro-Hun Therapy for your own awakening!

## Lydia Martin, West Palm Beach, FL

Ro-Hun has been a transformational process for me. Years of traditional psychotherapy prepared me but in no way come close to the healing and insight, indeed the transformation, that Ro-Hun, along with my relationship with my teacher and healer, have facilitated.

My life is continually enriched as I apply the lessons learned and utilize the tools given to me through Ro-Hun. Life can still be difficult, but I can always access Light. I no longer become stuck in the dark places of my soul. Instead, I move through them, bringing in Light and Love. Even in the midst of the dark places, I am now empowered to release negatives, keeping their life lessons but not their negative energy. My relationships are healthier and more stable. I am clearer on aspects of my life over which I have control, and I am able to more easily release those attachments that do not serve the greater good or me.

In the two years since my introduction to Ro-Hun, I've experienced pain, loss, and struggle, most significantly in my mother's passing and in the ongoing process of my husband's healing from colon cancer. As my mother transitioned, I was able to be fully present with her in her last days and through the grieving that followed, to heal long-held wounds and release attachments that otherwise would have threatened my sanity. As I become an elder, a matriarch, in my family, I find that I am empowered to live into those roles with grace and strength.

My husband, an Episcopal priest, continues his physical healing from cancer with chemotherapy, but more importantly, he is healing emotionally and spiritually. I am able to fully support him through this, whereas a few years ago, I would have crumbled under the weight of his illness and its implications. It is amazing to me that I can guide this holy man through his healing and transformational process; indeed, I find that I am growing and healing myself in the process. Watching my husband stretch and grow in body, mind, and spirit, to share in his healing and transformation, is indeed an ongoing gift. All of this is possible through my own experiences of healing and transformation through Ro-Hun.

My testimonial would not be complete without sharing thoughts on my own physical healing process, so closely entwined with my emotional and spiritual growth and healing. I struggled for more than 20 years with severe and debilitating back pain, fibromyalgia, and other limiting conditions. In Ro-Hun, I've found physical healing that multiple surgeries, countless procedures, and dozens of narcotics and medications could not bring about. I still experience pain and discomfort, but for the first time, it is manageable. I still take medications, but only a small fraction of what I once took. I find that by using the gifts and tools, the insights and inner wisdom, that Ro-Hun has opened me to, I am able to continually examine aches, pains, and other symptoms as they come up, to get "under" them to their emotional and spiritual roots, and to process and transform them, so that I am not so limited by them. This happens on many levels and, for me, is what true healing and transformation is all about.

Lastly, I find it hard to separate the healing power of Ro-Hun from the gifts of the healer, the Ro-Hun practitioner. I believe that each Ro-Hun practitioner is infused with wisdom and insight and empowered in their healing gifts. As the ripples from a duck's movements through water changes the nature of a lake, the healing and transformation Ro-Hun therapists share, empowers and enlightens those ministered to. They, in turn, go out and spread the Love and Light in their own circles. The ripples are far-reachng, carrying the Light of healing and transformation in an infinite stream. I am forever grateful to my therapist, to the process of Ro-Hun, to Patricia Hayes, and to the Divine for this healing and transformation in my life.

### Arnie Holtz, Palm City, FL

At age 40, I spent many months in traditional psychotherapy. Annoyed and bored, I finally ended my sessions but not without knowing what actions I needed to take to improve my life. At age 68, I have experienced the wonders of Purification, Caged, and Yhandi [author's note: Yhandi is an inner child/adult process that is separate from but complementary to Ro-Hun Therapy]. Now, I know *why* I needed to take those actions and *how* to continue improving my life. Life is still a mystery to me, but not as to myself and my relationship to All That Is. Powerful self-realization is Ro-Hun Therapy. Thank you to all my loving Ro-Hun therapists.

### Christine Malenda, Long Island, NY

Transcendental, life changing, healing for the mind, body and spirit—the gift of Ro-Hun in my life has been miraculous. Physical, mental, and emotional challenges have been overcome in as little as one session! Conditions that would have required surgery or life-long medication have truly vanished from my body. The empowerment of now knowing what can trigger my unique "buttons" and being able to overcome them every time is priceless. It has released me from fears, impossibilities, depression, and anxiety. Words feel too small to express the profound sacred journey that is Ro-Hun. My heart has new depth, my mind has new clarity and vitality for life, and love is now able to flow through me in a way I could never have imagined. I know of no greater gift for the person who is ready to let go of their suffering in any area of their life.

### Barbara Burk, RN, PhD, Ft. Wayne, IN

I came from a very abusive family. One brother tried to kill me, another brother sexually abused me from age three to eight, and my parents were physically, mentally, and emotionally abusive. From age 12 to 17, I tried to commit suicide five times.

I left home the night I received my high school diploma. From then on, everyone I attracted in my life was abusive. I didn't recognize it, though, because abuse was all I had known. I walked around with a big "V" on my chest for "Victim." Further, my mother taught me that sex was the only way to obtain and keep a relationship. So I did. I really didn't want to. But I didn't know any other way. Ultimately, I went through two marriages, both abusive, and abused my children, as well. When I ended up homeless after my first divorce and without a job to support my children, I resorted to using men again, which resulted in my second marriage.

During my second marriage, I became a nurse, but felt I should be doing something more. I asked the Source to show me my next step. The next day I received a flyer about Ro-Hun Therapy. I knew this was for me. I signed up for the class in March 2002. Through Ro-Hun, I gradually gained a healthier sense of myself. My eyes were opened to my husband's abuse and manipulation, and I knew I needed to leave. Because of the personal strength I'd achieved through

Ro-Hun, he found a force to be reckoned with! I was able to stand up for myself.

In 2007, I met my third husband. This time, there was no sexual manipulation from me because I had learned that I had value and he could love me for me. But I was afraid to marry again, afraid that he would change and become abusive. We dated for three and a half years, and during that time, I attended Delphi University and received my PhD in November 2010. In March 2011, Gilbert had a blood test, and the results were not good. We were married shortly after that test, and he passed away on December 22, 2011.

I really don't know what I would have done without knowing the tools that Ro-Hun gives you. Ro-Hun has helped me not only achieve a healthy sense of myself, but it has assisted me through my grieving process as well. It helped me to see and release the faulty thought that to keep the love alive you have to keep grief alive. It is such a relief that I don't have to tell our story anymore. I love Gilbert and always will, but the discovery of that faulty thought empowered me to move on with my life. I am not saying that I don't shed a few tears here and there, but I am no longer stuck in my grief.

Thanks to Ro-Hun, I have been able to release deep-seated fear, anger, worthlessness, manipulation, and powerlessness, and replace them all with strength and love. I make better choices. I love myself. I stand in my own energy, my own power. I no longer need the approval of anyone. Ro-Hun took the "V" off my chest. And I found my passion in life: empowering others.

### Rev. Carolyn Underwood, PhD, Mooresville, NC

What has Ro-Hun done for me? What hasn't it done for me! In 2002, I was in a very dark place in my life. I was what psychiatrists label "agoraphobic," and I suffered from severe free-floating anxiety. Anxiety was a mild term for what I experienced; my whole foundation had crumbled. I tried traditional therapy and medication for years; the therapy yielded very little results and the medication made me almost suicidal. At the time, I didn't realize that my main problem was a disconnection from my own spirit. I hadn't a clue who I was. For years, I tried to be what I thought I should be, mostly to please others. From the outside, I looked together, successful and happy, but inside I was slowly dying. In 1996, my "comfortable" rug was pulled out from under me. Plainly put, I had a nervous breakdown.

I searched for answers to my predicament, blaming illness, hormonal imbalances, and allergies. It took me a while to understand that it was mental, emotional, and spiritual. I proceeded to read every self-help book known to man and tried various modalities and processes that I thought would solve my life crisis dilemma. When I first learned of Ro-Hun Therapy, I approached it with skepticism; I thought it was just another empty scheme. In the next few weeks, Ro-Hun kept presenting itself to me, and honestly, I was becoming desperate for a cure, so I said "What the heck?" and scheduled an appointment. I had no idea what I was getting myself into, but I had to try. Quite honestly, I went to my first session with the expectation of failure, but the hope of success.

From the very first session, I felt a shift in my energy. Within a few months, I completed the basic Purification and Caged Processes. The insight, understanding, and healing I gained as a result of the Ro-Hun Processes was life altering. About six months after completing my sessions, I decided to attend Delphi University so that I could learn this transformational process to help others. You have to understand, six months prior to this decision, the thought of leaving my house, much less going all the way to Delphi University in Georgia, had been absolutely terrifying. Ro-Hun Therapy had literally transformed my life. I graduated the full program at Delphi University in 2010, and I am currently a Ro-Hun Doctor helping others just like myself. The beauty of this process is that it can help not only people like me, who are a mess, but it helps individuals whose lives are functioning fine, but who desire a stronger connection to the spirit.

If you had told me ten years ago that I would be doing what I am doing now, I would have called you nuts. Ro-Hun helped me to find myself, my purpose, and most of all, my connection to the universal source of all love and light. I now have a sense of fulfillment that I had never experienced in my life before.

### Alicia Keller, Nashville, TN

Ro-Hun therapy is a life-altering experience that transformed the way I view myself and the world I live in. Ro-Hun cracked me open and scrubbed my mental, emotional, and spiritual bodies clean of the nastiness and pain accumulated through lifetimes.

As a side note, when I first thought about what I should write, all I could think of was that without Ro-Hun, I would be dead, but that seemed a bit grim.

### Deryn Higgins, Doctor of Metaphysics, Ro-Hun Master, Bermuda

My experience with Ro-Hun has been very rewarding. When you take the Ro-Hun classes, everyone is a bit unsure at first, but when you start to identify the faulty thoughts and feelings and reactive selves that we hold onto, it's as if bells go off in everyone's head. They are so relieved to know they can release all this negativity and have a new way of thinking and feeling. There have been huge transformations that have taken place in my group Ro-Hun classes; it's a wonderful feeling to see all the students at the end of the class, each one a new person shining his or her light.

Working with people one on one with Ro-Hun has been an absolute joy. A chance to help someone make a change in his or her life and be there to guide without judgment is so amazing. Ro-Hun gives every person the opportunity to realize there is another way to live—and that it is really all about Love.

It really is all about love—loving the self enough to take courageous, effective healing steps; loving the people in our lives enough to see, understand, and forgive whatever has transpired. It is about loving a full, free, self-expressive life that opens the world to our creativity and inspiration and unites us with our beautiful Soul. In addition to the people who shared their experiences here, there are countless more across the United States and throughout the world who have found relief, expansion, and the joy of living through Ro-Hun Therapy.

Thus, it can be fully said without reservation, Ro-Hun Therapy is the greatest transformational process of our time.

# *Acknowledgements*

What would a Ro-Hun book be if there were no recognition of Dr. Ro-Hun and Patricia Hayes? Without that team trusting each other, this amazing process would not be part of our personal spiritual process. The world is a better place because of them. Thank you, Patricia, for your trust, willingness, and persistence to go beyond the limits to new and fertile ideas and methods. Your courage and dedication have helped set so many free.

Dr. Ro-Hun, thank you for your steadfastness in purpose and your desire to help mankind heal. Those of us who carry on your work are grateful for all you have taught us.

To my beloved late husband, Harry Hayes, I cannot thank you enough for your consistent, unwavering belief in me and my work. Without your strength, love, understanding, and sacrifice, my life as a Ro-Hun doctor would never have happened.

Without my colleagues—Judy Potter, Poochie Meyers, Nancy Smith, and Linda Griffith—my understanding of Ro-Hun would be profoundly thinner. Through our work together meeting each teaching challenge, this little band of instructors has deepened and broadened the power and effectiveness of Ro-Hun as a healing tool and way of life.

Judy, your wisdom and perception are legendary, as are your love and dedication to your clients. You are an inspiration to us all.

Poochie, your light touch, joy, and laughter lifted many a heavy moment to the Light, making healing happen more easily.

Nancy, your brilliance, clarity, and depth of knowledge are deeply inspiring, and your insights are accurate and healing.

Linda, your love shines in everything you do, lifting spirits and bringing Light.

Thank you all for your beautiful, loving, and dedicated hearts. You are the treasures in my treasure chest.

To Mary Beth Florentine, just when I needed you, you re-entered my life and undertook the task of the first editing of this work. Mary Beth, you gave me the push and encouragement to complete the writing. Thank you, endlessly.

Ultimately, I must acknowledge and thank all those wonderful, inspired, and talented Ro-Hun therapists who felt the power and transformative quality of Ro-Hun Therapy and chose this path as part of their healing ministries. Through your participation in class and in your healing work, you have taken Ro-Hun out into the world. Each of you is a seed of Light and Healing in a world of need. Each of you makes a difference. To all of you, I send my eternal love and gratitude.

# References

Arntz, William, Chasse, Betsy, and Vicente, Mark. (2007). What the Bleep Do We Know? HCI

Baron, Renee, and Wagele, Elizabeth, (1994). The Enneagram Made Easy. San Francisco, CA: HarperCollins,

Byrne, Rhonda. (2006). The Secret. New York: ATRIA Books

Chopra, Deepak. (1989). Quantum Healing. Bantam Books

Gray, John. (1984). What You Feel You Can Heal. Heart Publishing

Greene, Brian. (1999). The Elegant Universe. New York: W.W. Norton

Jung, Carl G., and REC Hull. (1981). The Archetypes and the Collective Unconscious (Collected works of CG Jung Vol. 9 Part I). Princeton, NJ: Princeton University Press

Latz, Dr. Tracy, and Ross, Marion. (2009). Shift: A Woman's Guide to Transformation. Morgan James Publishing

Lipton, Bruce. (2005). Biology of Belief. Hay House, Inc.

McVoy, Cullen. (1996). Finding Ro-Hun Awakening Through Spiritual Therapy. Montclair, NJ: Pooka Publications

Pert, Candace B. (1997). Molecules of Emotion. New York: Simon & Schuster

CPSIA information can be obtained
at www.ICGtesting.com
Printed in the USA
BVHW080232241221
624759BV00008B/632